DO-IT-YOURSELFER'S GUIDE TO
AUTO BODY
REPAIR & PAINTING

No. 949
$9.95

DO-IT-YOURSELFER'S GUIDE TO
AUTO BODY
REPAIR & PAINTING

By Charles R. Self

TAB BOOKS Inc.
BLUE RIDGE SUMMIT, PA. 17214

FIRST EDITION

FIRST PRINTING—SEPTEMBER 1978
SECOND PRINTING—MARCH 1979
THIRD PRINTING—APRIL 1980
FOURTH PRINTING—MARCH 1981

Library of Congress Cataloging in Publication Data

Self, Charles R.
    Do-it-yourselfer's guide to auto body repair & painting.

    Includes index.
    1. Automobiles—Bodies—Maintenance and repair. I. Title.
TL255.S37   629.2'6'028   77-18267
ISBN 0-8306-7949-9
ISBN 0-8306-6949-3 pbk.

Preface

Doing your own bodywork and painting makes more and more sense. New car prices rise every year and most of us, caught in the dollar bind, must keep our old cars running longer and longer. As the miles and years total up, rust and minor collision damage become inevitable. Farming the work out to a professional may cost more than the old buggy is worth. And the results may not be all that you hoped for.

Bodywork and painting require some skill, and there is little doubt that the best professional work cannot be matched by an amateur. But few professionals have the leisure to do their best. Working under time pressure the pro quickly learns to do the minimum that the customer will accept. Check out the average repair job and you'll see what I mean.

An amateur is free from this time pressure. It may take him longer to straighten a body panel but, if he has the patience, he can make a better job of it than the typical bodyshop. The same is true of paint, or at least of the relatively unsophisticated paints described in this book. Most of the work involved in a paint job is in the preparation; spraying the paint is almost of secondary concern, since there is some leeway to correct mistakes in the application.

It is impossible to predict costs: some readers will want to paint their car to stop rust; others will want a paint job deep enough to drown in. Whatever level of excellence you choose, you can be certain that your costs will be a tiny fraction of the bill a professional would hand you.

You will need a few specialized handtools and a decent spray gun and compressor. A professional-quality gun and tank-type compressor can be rented; the hand tools are relatively inexpensive. Paint costs vary. You can do an acceptable job with industrial enamel, although this paint does not have the durability of automotive finishes. The least expensive auto paint is old-fashioned, synthetic enamel. Acrylic enamel costs more than synthetic but dries quicker and is somewhat more forgiving, although an amateur will find overspray a problem. Most body shops use this paint. Next in sophistication and cost is acrylic lacquer. It dries very quickly—too quickly unless you're careful—and is intended to be laid on in multiple coats. Cost per gallon is higher than for acrylic enamel and coverage is poorer. But the results are spectacular. Other paints, such as cellulose lacquer and DuPont's Imron, have qualities that the average automobile does not need. Cellulose lacquer gives the deepest color of any known paint. It is used on limousines for heads of state, oil sheiks, and other notables. Since these gentlemen are unimaginative where car color is concerned, cellulose is only available in black and white. Imron and its competitors are frightfully expensive, but durable enough to be used on aircraft and ships. An Imron paint job will look as good in five years as the day you shoot it. And it looks very good.

Paul Dempsey

Contents

Acknowledgements

The list of people who have provided information and illustrations for this book is too long to include. But a few individuals and corporations have been extremely helpful, so my special thanks to John McCandless of Chrysler Corporation; Tom Roberts of Tom Gewant Ford/Lincoln/Mercury in Kerhonkson, New York; Joe Bailey at Gewant Ford; Ford Motor Company; Cleanweld Products, Inc., and Charles Muirhead; Lee Sunsted at Century Manufacturing; Ditzler Automotive Refinishes and Don Desautels; Sherwin-Williams; Chuck Thorne at Montgomery Ward; and quite a few other people.

Charles R. Self

Hand Tools

1

While tools are considered important to bodywork, they are a long way from being the only items you will have to pay a great deal of attention to while working on your car. Still, without the proper tools used in the correct manner there is little chance you will be able to complete the work you wish to do.

In many cases, the tools will seem strange if you're used to working mostly with wrenches, screwdrivers, and tuneup equipment, though a great many of them will seem familiar to the veteran woodworker. Your job in auto bodywork is to straighten and shape metal, much as a cabinetmaker forms wood. Some of the tools will seem similar, though the working material is different.

The condition of your tools, their quality, their correctness for the job at hand, and their proper use all make very heavy contributions to the quality and appearance of the finished work.

HAMMERS

While the standard ball peen hammer sees more than a little use during many jobs, the hammers associated with changing the shape of battered sheet metal may look distinctly odd to the layman. These are called dinging or bumping hammers and are used in conjunction with a tool called a bumping dolly. Their only reason for existence is the removal of low and high spots from relatively thin sheet metal.

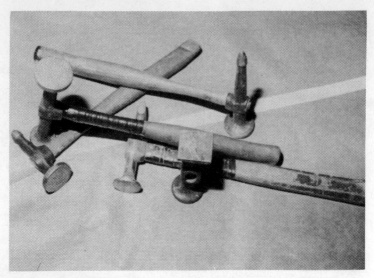

Fig. 1-1. Assorted hammers, with a crosshatched shrinking hammer on the left.

Used with the proper dolly as backup much like a blacksmith's anvil, the hammer is swung with a series of light blows to remove dents of various sizes.

Dinging hammers may have round or square faces, and those faces can be flat or slightly convex, depending on the job. Round hammers with flat faces are for general dent removal, while square hammers are used for working in close to body seams, beads, and various accessories attached to the body.

Hammer head length—the distance from the handle socket to the face—will vary a great deal. Some dinging hammers have 4-inch heads, while others have heads as long as 6 inches. The reason for the variation is simple: If the space you have to swing the hammer is only 6 inches wide, you won't get much action out of a dinging hammer with a 6-inch long head!

Pick hammers have both ends terminating in a point; combination hammers combine a pick with a conventional face. Pick hammers are used to remove dents too small to be handled with the standard dinging hammer and dolly block. Weights, head length, and pick sharpness vary widely in order to fit the job. Figure 1-1 shows a selection of bodywork hammers.

Heavier hammers, called roughing hammers, are frequently used to slam a major dent back into some approximation of the original panel shape before the dinging or pick hammers are unlimbered. Roughing hammers are seldom used with dollies, though many bodyworkers prefer to back up the sheet metal with a two by four.

Looking otherwise like a standard dinging hammer, the shrinking hammer has a crosshatched face and is used for shrinking sheet metal that has expanded too much under the dinging hammer and bumping dolly (shrinking is done in conjunction with heat applied from an oxy-acetylene torch).

Bell peen, or mechanics', hammers, are used for a variety of jobs, from driving a chisel to cutting rivets or screws and bolts, to setting those rivets, to punching out drift pins, and so on.

SPOONS AND DOLLY BLOCKS

Spoons and dolly blocks are backing devices for dinging hammers. They are small anvils upon which the sheet metal is beaten back into shape. The spoonhead or the bumping dolly is held on the side opposite that being hammered. The hammer is then struck against the metal with sharp, though not hard, blows. The spoon, with its long handle, can also serve as a pry bar to spring metal back closer to its original shape before hammering. When a spoon is used as a dolly block, it is generally inserted into those places where a dolly block either won't fit or can't be held.

Dolly blocks come in many different shapes and sizes to match the desired contour of the metal being straightened as closely as possible. The better the match, the easier the final work will be, of course. Spoons come in different profiles.

Spoons are a time saver. They fit through access holes in doors and can be snaked around panel and check-lid braces.

Pry bars, whether part of a spoon or not, are useful tools, for they allow the bodyworker to align fender-mounting brackets, door, hood and trunk hinges, often without removing of the door, hood or trunk. Pry bars come in many shapes and sizes with some designed exclusively for auto work. Figure 1-2 illustrates a few types of dolly blocks and spoons.

FILES

Ordinary files can be used though there is no substitute for a body file (Fig. 1-3). The blade is flexible and secured in a special

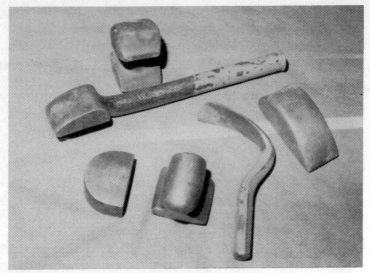

Fig. 1-2. Spoons and dolly blocks.

holder. Also of great help, especially when working plastic body fillers, are open files, known as "cheese graters" because of their resemblance to that kitchen utensil. Since body filler is best worked before it has hardened, an open file is necessary to allow the strands of material to fall away without clogging the teeth. Other files, the

Fig. 1-3. Body file in use.

flexible models, conform to the curves of the body panel and are most often used to provide an indication of where to continue dinging or filling. The high spots show as shiny, and can then be dinged down (or the lower spots can be filled, if the surface is being raised).

SOLDER PADDLES

Maple paddles used to smooth lead on a body panel have various blade profiles (Fig. 1-4). A bodyworker with much experience may use only a single paddle, one that he is comfortable with.

PULL RODS AND SUCTION CUPS

Pull rods are a time saver. Often it is necessary to remove a great deal of interior trim, padding, and such to get a pry bar into position. In many cases, the pull rod can be used on the outside of the panel. Pull rods come in two forms: A simple rod that has a collet at its end that will hold either a screw or hook; and a more complicated unit that has its own sliding hammer on the shaft to provide more power for popping out dents.

Shallow creases and dents are the damage most easily removed with pull rods. A series of holes is drilled along the crease (usually 9/64 inch in diameter) 1 or 2 inches apart. The pull rod is inserted in each hole and pulled, or hammered back. The crease or dent will gradually lift. The rod without the slide hammer has more authority when it is in conjunction with a dinging hammer.

For extremely shallow dents that extend over a large area, the bodyworker's suction cup can prove to be a time saver (Fig. 1-5). The suction cup is wetted and placed on the dented surface. A good

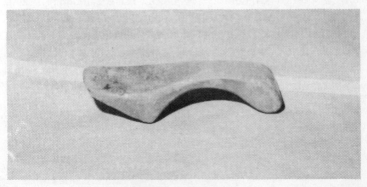

Fig. 1-4. Solder paddle.

Fig. 1-5. Suction cup for shallow dents.

heave will often pop the dent out. This tool can be used only on large panels, such as roofs. Other types of panels are often too well braced to return to shape so easily.

The same type of suction cup is used as an aid in removing windshields and rear windows.

MECHANIC'S TOOLS

More conventional mechanic's tools are also essential for work on an automobile body. Many screws, nuts, and bolts must be removed in the course of major bodywork. Thus, the bodyworker needs a selection of sockets, open- and box-end wrenches, screwdrivers, pliers, and other tools. Among the handiest tools are locking pliers. Best known of these are Vise Grips but Channellock makes pliers they call TogLLock that I consider superior. You will also need a supply of wet-and-dry sandpaper in various grits (the higher the number on the sandpaper, the finer the grit, and grits for bodywork go all the way up to No. 600).

SPECIAL TOOLS

Door handles, window winders, and body trim usually require special tools for removal. These tools are easily found in local automobile supply stores, and most of them carry the K-D brand. K-D Manufacturing Company (Lancaster, PA 17604) specializes in tools for uses not generally foreseen by the companies that produce the wrenches you can buy at a hardware store. Figure 1-6 shows a pair of K-D door-handle and window-crank removal tools. Prices are reasonable and quality is in the good-to-excellent range.

Here's a point to think about: Consider the quality of the tool you are buying carefully. If you plan to make a one-time repair on your car, try to borrow or rent tools. You will have to buy some tools, but *do* spring for top quality. If, on the other hand, you plan to repair your car, your friend's car, and go on to some customizing work, consider the top-of-the-line companies. Snap-On is the name most mechanics use when tools are praised (though Proto and S & K come in for their share, and Sears' Craftsman tools are used by more professional mechanics than most people would believe). You won't be able to find a store dealing in Snap-On tools, though. They are sold through independent dealers, who truck around to garages, dealerships, and manufacturers to take orders. You will have to

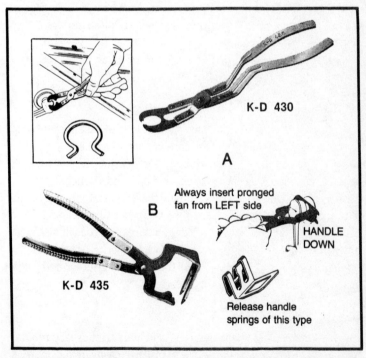

Fig. 1-6. K-D door-handle and molding-clip tools. No. 430 is for Ford and GM production using the clip shown (view A); No. 435 is for Chrysler production (view B).

make friends with a mechanic and order through him to get the Snap-On line.

From this point, it's but a short jump into the more expensive tools such as arc welders, oxy-acetylene welding outfits, compressors, and spray guns. These will be discussed in other chapters.

Using Hand Tools

Simply describing the hand tools needed for automobile bodywork may help you when purchasing time arrives, but to really get into the work, proper techniques must be learned. Unfortunately a description serves only to get you started. After that, it's up to you to practice those basics. The more you practice the better you will become, but during all the preliminary hammering, dinging, and filing, it is a good idea to remember that the final job will be easier and more professional looking because of the time you are putting in now.

USING DINGING HAMMERS AND DOLLY BLOCKS

Because the first phase of most bodywork requires extensive use of bumping hammers and dolly blocks, I will begin with them. At the start, hold the dolly block in one hand and the hammer in the other. Insert the dolly block behind the panel you wish to reshape.

There are two ways of using the dolly behind the sheet metal as you wield the hammer: If the hammer is struck directly on the dolly radius (with the sheet metal intervening, of course), you are doing what is known as dinging on the dolly (Fig. 2-1). If the dolly, while still held directly under the dent or crease, is not centered under the hammer blows, you are dinging off the dolly (Fig. 2-2). You will notice that the dolly remains in place behind the dent or crease; the hammer strikes either above the dolly or on one side of it.

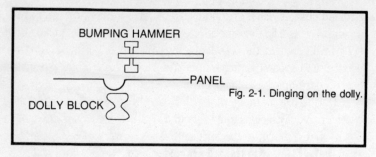

BUMPING HAMMER

PANEL

DOLLY BLOCK

Fig. 2-1. Dinging on the dolly.

In either case, it is essential that the dolly conform to the basic curve of the panel (Fig. 2-3). Your hammer must have the correct profile. Using the flat face of a dinging hammer on a concave panel leaves nicks and dents that will have to be filled with lead or epoxy. You are going to have to use some filler but the best bodyworkers are distinguished by the small amount of filler necessary to smooth out their hammer work. For concave surfaces, a concave hammer is necessary for top results. Flat and convex surfaces require a flat hammer.

Select a dolly to fit the curve of the bodywork, making sure that the dolly's radius is slightly smaller than the panel curve.

Hammer strokes are important. A properly swung dinging hammer can make the job go easier. An improperly wielded hammer will add to the work or, in extreme cases, can ruin the entire job. Body metal is relatively fragile stuff, even under the impacts generated by a light dinging hammer. It may be satisfying to feel a solid thunk every time you swing that hammer but such treatment is almost certain to stretch the panel. The face of the hammer must make solid, square contact with the panel. If not, the edges of the hammer will nick the sheet metal.

A dinging hammer cannot be used in the same manner that a carpenter's hammer is used. A bent nail costs only a few cents, while

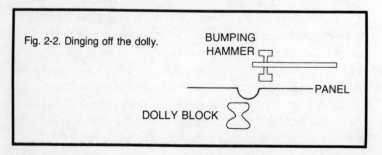

Fig. 2-2. Dinging off the dolly.

BUMPING HAMMER

PANEL

DOLLY BLOCK

a ruined quarter panel or fender can add hundreds of dollars to the repair bill. Use a light-to-moderate slapping action, while holding the dolly firmly behind the surface being struck. If the dolly tends to bounce, and doesn't return immediately to the panel, you are striking too hard or else holding the dolly improperly.

Dollies are nothing more than a form-fitted backup for the hammer. A dolly block should rebound slightly from each blow. Dolly blocks that conform to the surface being worked can be held in the palm of the hand, with the fingers folded back, although the tips can be placed on the surface to facilitate rebound—as Tom Roberts is doing in Fig. 2-4. Hold the dolly with moderate pressure. You may get hand cramps at first, since the hand absorbs some of the shock, but the cramps soon pass.

USING SPOONS

Spoons are less simple to handle than dolly blocks only because they can be used to do more jobs. When a spoon is serving as a dolly block in a hard-to-reach spot, such as inside a door, the same precautions apply to spoon use as to dolly use. The spoon must fit the radius of the panel and must rebound to the proper spot each time the hammer strikes. Because of the long handle on many spoons, you will find it difficult to control the rebound. For the inexperienced worker, then, a much slower hammer rhythm is recommended.

The lighter spoons can be used to spread the effect of hammering over a wide area. When the damaged area is ridged, the spoon is placed on top of the ridge and struck with a dinging hammer to spread the blow over the surface. Because the blows are unbacked, take care to keep from deforming the metal any more than it already has been.

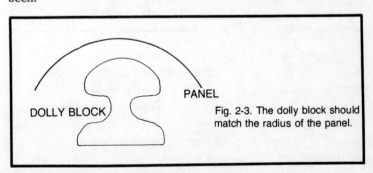

PANEL

DOLLY BLOCK

Fig. 2-3. The dolly block should match the radius of the panel.

Fig. 2-4. Tom Roberts bumps a Granada hood lip. When Tom was done, the metal was nearly as smooth as the original.

Spoons used as dolly blocks should not be tightly held. Your hand should act only as a guide—sort of a position reference—to bring the spoon back to the correct spot for the next blow.

To use the spoon as a pry bar, the basics of leverage are really all that need to be remembered. With that, and a bit of careful thought as to what piece will bend where, all you need to do is find a fulcrum and pry.

USING PICK HAMMERS

The pick hammer differs in more than looks from the dinging hammer. The pick on one end of the head, along with the dinging hammer on the other end, make this an extremely versatile tool, though the versatility for any particular job depends upon the size of the pick. The smaller the dent to be picked, the smaller the size of the pick used. Pick hammers are often used without dolly blocks, but for the novice a dolly block is recommended.

This hammer can be used freehand with the dolly or it can be held in place and struck with a ball peen hammer. This second method is best for the beginning bodyworker, since it reduces the chances of missing the small target.

Pick hammers can be used to force out dents in spots where a dolly or spoon cannot be used. Typically, this will be in a lower section of a door or adjacent to trunk and body braces.

Pick hammers, if used properly—and that means gently—work quite well without a dolly block. But you are advised to practice on a spare chunk of sheet metal before trying the real thing.

USING BODY FILES

Body files are most often used to locate high and low spots in the hammered metal, rather than as tools to take off large amounts of metal. The file is too coarse to use for metal removal on the thin sheet metal used in automobile bodies, and it works too rapidly to use on lead or plastic fillers. Body metal is about 1/32 in. thick.

Properly used, a body file is very handy but improperly used, the same tool is a quick route to a ruined panel. Move the file in the direction of the flattest point on the panel, shifting it slightly to one side during each stroke. Make the stroke several inches shorter than the file is long for best control, and start each stroke with the front of the file blade in contact with the metal. This gives the rocking motion best suited for curved panels (almost all body panels have some curve to them). The strokes should be light, doing little more than skimming the surface of the metal.

The cheese grater shown on the left in Fig. 2-5 is used for shaping epoxy filler. The filler should be built up slightly higher than the original panel. While the material is still fairly soft, move the cheese grater across the work, using the same technique that you would for a standard body file.

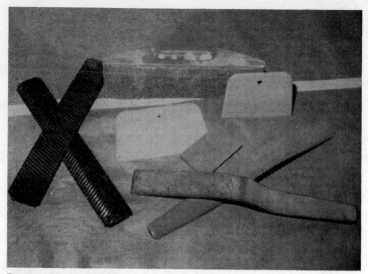

Fig. 2-5. Body files (left); sanding block (top center); squeegees (center, top right), and bumping files.

SMALL POWER TOOLS

With the above coverage of specialized handtools, we turn to the power tools needed to produce a professional-looking job. One of the most important of these tools is a portable grinder (Fig. 2-6). A grinder will save time at a half dozen places along the way to a

Fig. 2-6. Using a power grinder to locate high spots on truck fender.

finished repair, including the last step of waxing and buffing the completed (and cured) paint job.

Unfortunately grinders are expensive. While a backing plate and sanding disc chucked in a drill motor is a substitute, it is not the real thing. Consideration should be given to getting past the $150 price tag placed on these tools. One way is to pick up a used grinder from a body shop. Minor repairs, made at home, can sometimes bring the tool back to life. If you go this route, make certain that the shop will refund at least part of your money if the grinder proves to be unsalvageable.

Most amateur bodyworkers go with a sander/buffer head on a drill motor as shown in Fig. 2-7. If this is your intention, try to locate

Fig. 2-7. Using a 3M grinder to locate high and low spots on short radius curve.

a good quality, right-angle attachment for the disc. The attachment will give better control than the usual direct drive. The more powerful the drill motor, the better. Quarter-inch drills are not powerful enough for heavy grinding, but quality 3/8-inch drills are, and the better cost only a few dollars more than the smaller, less versatile, drill motors. Still, consider at least renting, if not buying, a grinder/buffer/polisher such as the machine shown in Fig. 2-6.

Sanding discs come in a variety of diameters; the most used size with the power grinder is 7 inches, and 5 inches for drill motors. Grit size is described by number, such as grit No. 60. That number refers to the size hole in a screen that the grit will pass through. The higher the grit number, the smaller the grit size. No. 16 is for coarse work such as paint removal, while No. 60 would be used for fine metal finishing—don't confuse grinder grit numbers with sandpaper numbers, though the progression is the same. Sandpapers for finish work range from No. 200 to No. 600. Open- and closed-coat discs are available. Open-coat discs are the more versatile of the two for paint removal, since the widely spaced grits are slower to clog. Closed-coat discs are more useful for metal removal because they have more grit on their surfaces and cut more rapidly.

Epoxy body fillers often require the use of open-coat grinding discs at the outset of the job, before curing is complete, and closed-coat discs for the final finishing and smoothing operations.

Unless you are familiar with bodyworking tools, purchase a scrapped hood or trunk lid from a wrecking yard.

The first step in learning to use a grinder involves taking the paint off the panel down to bare metal. Select an open-coat disc and set the grinder up. Use side-to-side strokes holding the machine at a slight angle. The backing disc should flex slightly as you apply pressure.

You can use a maul to knock a few dents in the hood or deck lid. Use the grinder with a closed-coat disc, and a side-to-side stroke, to locate high and low spots (just as you would do with a body file). Once the low spots have been picked up, you can move on to practice in featheredging the painted sections with a general-use grit (about a No. 24). From there, it's only necessary to get some practice in fine finishing with a No. 36 disc.

After the basic finishing is done, you can move on to a No. 60 grit (closed-coat) disc and practice bringing the metal to an almost buffed finish. The grinder is not tilted as much as when paint is cut, since a larger portion of the pad should be in contact with the work surface. Buffing smoothes the scratches left by the coarse and general-duty discs. If the job were to go on from here, primer/surfacer would now be applied.

Tools are inherently dangerous. When power is added, the danger becomes serious. A grinder should be handled with care because the edge of the disc can cause nasty wounds. Clothing should be reasonably snug so it cannot catch and wind on the disc (scarfs, ties and the like are verboten around all power tools). Eye protection is essential when working with a grinder, as it is with any other power tool that throws chips.

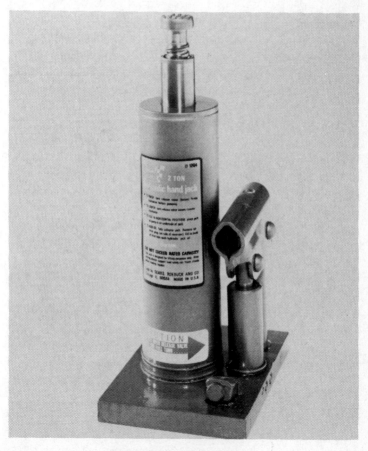

Fig. 2-8. Sears hydraulic jack.

AROUND-THE-CAR SAFETY

Few consider safety when doing automobile work at home. Too many people think of an automobile as a familiar object, and treat it with at least a degree of contempt, especially when it is stationary. This attitude can have tragic consequences.

First the no smoking rule should be enforced. Bodywork involves flammable materials—body cleaners, paints, thinners, and reducers.

All safety precautions, including being very careful of water puddles when electrical tools are used, should be followed. The reason for the emphasis on the puddle problem is the need for wet sanding as the job progresses. Wet sanding should be done by hand, unless power tools operate by compressed air. Much of this work will be done in home garages, I'm sure, and if your garden hoses are like mine, they manage to drip for days after the faucet is shut down. Some of the water can be picked up with a wet/dry vacuum cleaner, and should be, but take the extra precaution of wearing rubber-soled shoes. Be sure tools are double insulated or properly grounded.

Fig. 2-9. Sears scissors jack.

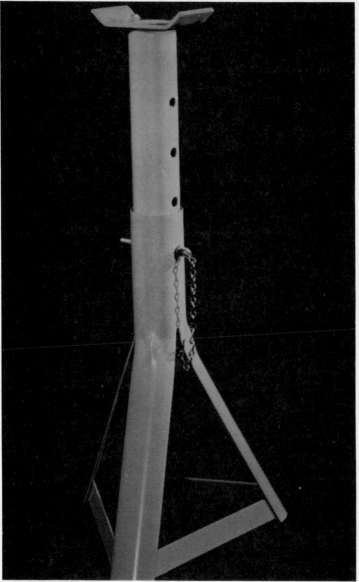

Fig. 2-10. Sears jack stands are essential to safe undercar work.

Perhaps the greatest danger is the off-the-floor automobile supported with a bumper jack. The best favor you can do yourself is to file the original equipment jack in the trash.

Either a small hydraulic jack, shown in Fig. 2-8, or a mechanical scissors jack, shown in Fig. 2-9, is safer. But even properly placed

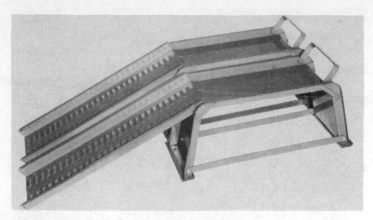

Fig. 2-11. Sears ramps.

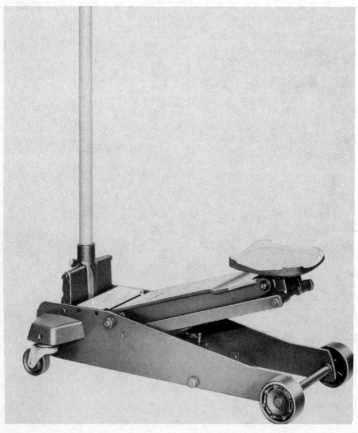

Fig. 2-12. Sears hydraulic floor jack.

(under the rear axle or under a front A-frame) jacks are not safe for undercar work. This applies whether you are crawling all the way under the automobile, or working within a wheel well to install fender flares.

Once the car is jacked to the height you need, you should slip jack stands under the frame or axle to solidly support the car. Always check, first visually and then by giving the car a couple of good shoves, that the vehicle is firmly planted on the jack stands. Stands of the type shown in Fig. 2-10 can be extended to provide enough working room for most jobs.

For those who need to lift only a single end of the automobile, the drive-on stands shown are excellent substitutes for jackstands and provide an even firmer base for the car. They are more expensive, and limit the car to a fixed height, but a nice feature of these Sears models is the detachable ramps that allow the worker greater freedom of movement than the permanent ramps (Fig. 2-11).

The ultimate in jacks is the hydraulic floor jack shown in Fig. 2-12. These tools are expensive but do a superb and safe job of lifting large loads and can be adapted to engine and transmission removal.

Welding Equipment

3

Brazing and heat shrinking are the primary uses of welding equipment for auto bodywork. Occasionally the bodyworker will need to do a bit of fusion welding and cutting. Gas torches can also be used for melting body lead that is sometimes used instead of plastic fillers.

Gas and electric welders each have their special uses. As an example, while an arc welder can be used to cut sheet metal, an oxy-acetylene torch is easier to use for this purpose. On the other hand, an arc welder is useless for spreading lead body filler, while an oxy-acetylene torch works well if used carefully. Those lacking experience would find a propane torch superior to either because the amount of heat generated is seldom enough to cause panel warping.

Metal shrinking requires heat, a bumping hammer, and a dolly block to restore a body panel to a shape more nearly its original after repeated hammer and dolly work has thinned and stretched metal.

The job may sound easy, and can even look easy when done by an expert, but for the beginner, heat shrinking is almost impossible. Shrinking is a job where the feel is more important than anything else. Measurements and coil upon coil of patience are of only minimal assistance. Care should be exercised to keep panel stretch to a minimum.

Because of its greater versatility, we'll start off with a look at gas welding equipment. Gas welding, as used for automotive bodywork, invariably refers to oxygen-acetylene welding, although the welder may use a fuel gas other than acetylene. Propane produces less heat than acetylene, and is the fuel used in the Cleanweld-Solidox outfit (Fig. 3-1). This device is much less expensive than full-size oxy-acetylene outfits, especially the really good, two-stage models.

In passing it should be mentioned that the term "inert gas welding" refers to electric arc welding. TIG (tungsten-inert-gas) and MIG (metal-inert-gas) welding equipment and techniques shield the arc with inert gas, making it possible to weld chromemoly steel, magnesium, aluminum and other difficult metals.

OXY-ACETYLENE WELDING EQUIPMENT

Welding oxygen is 99 1/2 % pure, with a half a percentage point of nitrogen remaining. Oxygen is not flammable, but it willingly supports combustion in other substances and requires a great deal of care in handling. Oxygen will spontaneously burst into flame upon contact with grease and oil.

Like oxygen, acetylene is a colorless gas, but differs in that it is combustible. Acetylene is stored in pressure vessels containing a solvent that holds many times its own weight in acetylene.

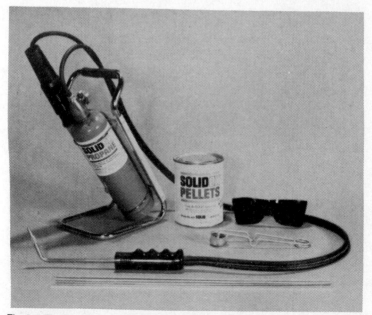

Fig. 3-1. The Solidox oxy-propane kit is a logical choice for the home bodyworker or substitute for the real thing.

Propane is derived from petroleum and finds its major use as a fuel gas in brazing and shrinking applications. Since the heat produced is not as great as with acetylene, the amateur may well find propane the fuel gas of his choice.

WELDING RODS

Welding rods are used to add metal to the weld. Welding rods must match, as closely as possible, the properties of the metal being welded.

Welding rod sizes and compositions vary with diameters from 1/16 inch to 3/8 inch. Mild steel rod is best for auto bodies.

FLUXES

Welding fluxes are used to remove the contaminants from the surfaces being welded. These contaminants present a serious problem and vary in composition from simple oils and greases to certain oxides. Fluxes handle both types of contamination, although the metal to be welded should be free of paint, rust, and oily fingerprints.

Fluxes are applied in several ways. Powdered flux requires the heated tip of the welding rod be dipped into the can of flux, though it may also be applied directly to the surface of the metal being welded. Powdered flux is difficult for the novice to use, since the can is hard to see when you are working from behind dark goggles. Paste or liquid fluxes are applied directly to the metal being welded and are easier for the amateur to use.

THE TORCH

Acetylene and oxygen are mixed at the torch. When the mixture is ignited, it burns at the end of the welding tip attached to the torch. The flame produced by the burning mixture is directed at the materials to be welded until the area to be joined reaches the temperature where fusion welding can occur (for brazing, the temperature need not be as high, and for cutting, a different tip is used).

Oxy-acetylene welding torches are made up of a handle, a mixing chamber, extensions, and a torch tip. Valve assemblies are found at the rear of the handle, and may be either a permanent part of the assembly or detachable.

For tank welding, that is, where tanks containing oxygen and acetylene are used, an equal-pressure torch is used. The gasses pass through their separate hoses—the hoses should never be mixed around—into separate pipes at the handle, from whence they go on into the mixer, or mixing chamber. The mixer serves not only to mix the two gasses, but also works as a device to prevent flashback through the torch and into the lines or tanks. Without this flashback prevention feature, many welders would not be here today. The mixed gasses flow through the extension and to the welding tip. The welding tip is sized to give the proper amount of heat for the job.

For most auto bodywork a No. 00 tip is sufficient. Almost never does automotive welding require a tip larger than No. 5.

When the regulator is being connected to the tanks, you will notice that the threads for the oxygen inlet are sized differently than those at the acetylene inlet. This is a safety feature, and is extended to the hose outlets, where the oxygen hose has a right-hand thread and the acetylene hose a left-hand thread. It is impossible, or nearly so, to hook the tanks to the wrong hoses and generate a sheet of flame where it is not at all welcome. Of course, Murphy's Law states that sooner or later someone is going to do something wrong, no matter how difficult it is. Forcing the connections can get a semblance of a hookup on the wrong hoses and tanks: Don't. If you have to force anything on an oxy-acetylene welding outfit, you are either doing something wrong (and dangerous) or the unit is broken, mismanufactured, or generally fouled up. Have any needed repairs made before continuing.

A two-stage regulator is not essential and is more expensive than a single-stage regulator. But as pressure drops in the cylinders, a single-stage regulator requires frequent adjustment to keep the torch flame constant. While the pressure drop is predictable, the continuing interruption of the work can drive you bonkers. It seems worthwhile to spend the extra money for a two-stage regulator, which not only compensates for the loss of tank pressure, but is also less likely to freeze up than a single-stage regulator. Freezing at the oxygen valve seat causes fluctuations of line pressure and makes flame control difficult.

ARC WELDING EQUIPMENT

An arc welder will expand your work horizons considerably: Arc welding is stronger and safer than oxy-acetylene welding. An arc

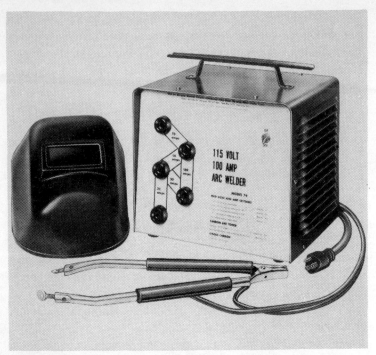

Fig. 3-2. The Century 100-amp arc welder is adequate for light welding.

welder in the proper hands will do nearly everything that a gas welder will do. Anyone interested in serious body and frame work should invest in both types of welding equipment.

Arc welding equipment comes in all sizes and shapes. Fortunately the choice of the rig is simplified by the narrow requirements of automotive bodywork. To begin, you won't need a direct current arc welder. Since an alternating current machine is the alternative, you then should consider the size of the welder. To simplify things, 100-amp "cracker boxes" are too small for general work (Fig. 3-2). If you will never do anything but weld sheet metal, though, 100 amps might be sufficient. The maximum that you will need is 200 or 300 amps. While a 200-ampere model might be on the low side, a 250-amp machine such as Century 250 AC/DC shown in Fig. 3-3 will handle any automotive job—if allowed a bit of rest every 10 or 15 minutes. For surplus capacity, consider a 295-amp model such as shown in Fig. 3-4.

Some arc welders have features that make life easier for the home craftsman. Ward's Powr Kraft 230 Amp AC/DC machine has a heat-selection panel that takes the guesswork out of choosing the rod and heat range for the job (Fig. 3-5). Once the rod is selected to match the type and thickness of the metal to be welded, the heat-range selector is turned to the number on the panel that corresponds

Fig. 3-3. Century's new development—a consumer-size AC/DC welding machine.

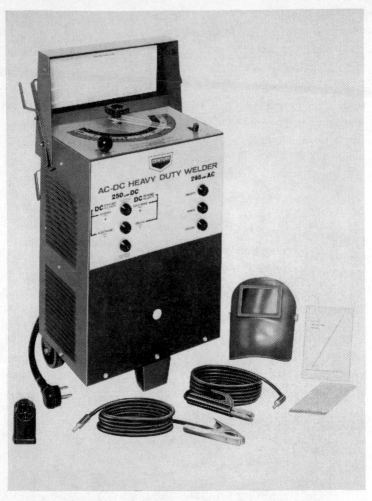

Fig. 3-4. The Century 250-amp AC/DC welder and accessories.

to that rod. This outfit, including electrode and ground cables, input cable, and a full-face helmet should arrive at your home for a little more than $200 at this writing. A comparable two-stage oxy-acetylene outfit costs about $15 less. But the gas welder requires two additions, one an absolute essential, and one that I consider handy enough to be worth five time the cost. First, you must secure oxygen and acetylene tanks, at a cost of at least $150. Second, a hand truck for those cylinders can save sore muscles and broken regulators. Total cost, then, for an oxy-acetylene outfit can run to about $400. Of course, the tanks can be rented at far less initial cost. Actually, what you are doing is buying the tanks over a perio dof years, as they weaken with use and must eventually be discarded. Oxy-acetylene welding sets are available for less, of course, and there are always Solidox oxy-propane welding rigs. These tiny rigs feed from oxygen pellets, or candles, and propane. There isn't enough heat produced for heavy-duty welding, but there is enough for other jobs, such as brazing. The price ranges from $35 to $50, depending on where you buy.

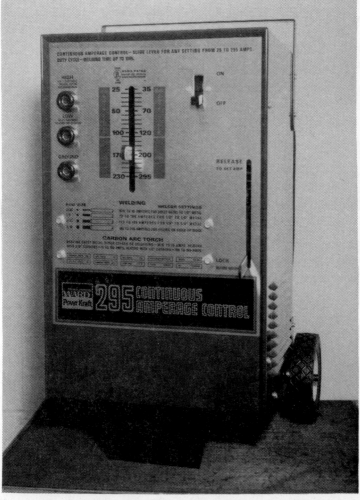

Fig. 3-5. Montogomery Ward's 230-amp AC/DC arc welder.

One form of welder that should be avoided at all costs is the nickel-dime unit described in newspaper ads as an arc welder. Usually sold only by mail, these $25 specials cannot come close to producing the hot arc needed for fusion welding, and most present an electroshock hazard.

If you decide you want an arc welder, make sure you get the best you can afford, whether new or used. Get at least a 200-amp capacity, and make sure it is listed by both the Underwriter's Laboratories and the National Electrical Manufacturers' Association. For power you will need a 220-volt service capable of handling at least 9000 watts (50-60 amp fusing).

WELDING RODS

Arc welding rods must be matched to the job. Flux-coated rods are your best bet, though they cost more than rods that have to be dipped into powdered or paste flux. Special rods allow you to cut and weld cast iron (even the weld will be machineable), sheet metal, and aluminum (get plenty of practice first). Some will give a reasonably strong weld through dirt and rust, though this last is certainly not for critical applications.

ACCESSORIES

Sundry tools for the arc welder include the arc torch, used for heating, soldering, and brazing. The arc torch employs two carbon rods to produce an arc which can then be used to heat the surface being worked. This torch, with considerable practice, can be used to heat and shrink metal, too, though an oxy-acetylene outfit remains the tool of choice for this application.

Weld-cleaning tools are essential with both gas and arc welders. As a bead is laid, slag bubbles to the top. It must be removed before any subsequent bead is laid, and before the weld can be painted or plated. Chipping hammers and wire brushes are used to dislodge the slag, with the chipping hammer and wire brush often combined in a single, very useful tool.

Welding Techniques

This chapter discusses electric and gas welding techniques.

ARC WELDING

Arc welding is one of a group of fusion welding processes in which an electric arc is formed between the work surface and an electrode, or welding rod. Once the arc is formed, the temperature rises to 6500 ° F.

Heat from the arc produces a small puddle of molten metal on the work surface, which will provide, if properly handled, the welder with what are known as tack welds. For fusion welding along seams and over larger areas, additional material is added from the electrode as it melts.

Arc welding seems simple, for so long as the arc is maintained, the welding rod is matched to the work at hand and the machine's heat range is correct, little should go wrong. Unfortunately, things are not this simple.

Safety Precautions

Have a licensed electrician inspect the wiring: Fuse and circuit rating must be adequate for the machine and the return circuit must be grounded to National Electrical Code standards.

- Be positive that ventilation is adequate so that welding fumes escape rather than hover around the welder. Use a fan if needed.

- Do not place electrode holders down so that they come in contact with any grounded conductor surface.
- Do not weld fuel tanks and other containers that have held volatile substances.
- Cut away from you to reduce the chances of molten metal spraying your face or clothing.
- Ultraviolet radiation from the arc will burn exposed skin and will blind unshielded eyes. Wear the appropriate protective gear.

Protective Gear

The helmet supplied with the machine is far from professional quality, although it is adequate with the proper lens. Professional helmets are comfortable, well balanced in the up or down positions, and feature splatter-proof lens covers. Ordinary lens covers are soon ruined by splatter accumulations, particularly when worn by the novice who tends to produce fireworks.

The lens—the dark window in the helmet—is rated by the amount of light it filters. The higher the number, the darker the lens. A No. 10 lens is adequate for general work with a 5/32-inch diameter electrode. No. 12 is for 1/4-inch electrodes and No. 14, the most opaque that you will use, is for serious work with 5/16-inch electrodes.

Wear leather gauntlets and a long-sleeved cotton or duck shirt, buttoned to the neck. Avoid synthetic fibers—nylon, Orlon, and most others have very low melting points and increase the danger of splatter burns.

Hook Up

Once these safety essentials are taken care of, the welding machine can be plugged in. Connect the ground clamp from the welder to the work being welded. Your connection here must be resistance-free; otherwise the ground clamp will overheat, making it difficult to maintain an arc. Clean away rust, scale, paint, and grease that might affect the ground.

Heat Ranges

Select a clean, dry welding rod of appropriate composition for the metals to be welded and insert it firmly in the electrode holder.

WELDING		ROD SIZE	AMPS SETTING
Mild Steel, Up to ⅛"Metal		3/32"	Min.— 90
Mild Steel, Up to ¼" Metal		1/8"	70 — 160
Mild Steel, ¼" and Thicker (Limited input welders)		5/32"	120 — 180
Mild Steel, ½" and Thicker (Industrial type welders)		3/16"	170 — 240
Hard Steel (Use stainless steel rod when in doubt about the hardness of your metal.)			
Up to ⅛" Metal		3/32"	50 — 100
⅛" and Heavier Metal		1/8"	90 — 150
Cast Iron (Weld a little, cool a lot, in beads about 1" long, followed by light peening.)			
Nickel Rod Is Easy to Work and Machinable.		3/32"	50 — 70
Cast Iron Rod Is Harder to Work, and Non-Machinable.		1/8"	80 — 120
Hard Surface (Hold medium long arc, let rod "spray.")		1/8"	80 — 140
Cutting — Standard Welders		1/8"	Max.
Heavy Duty Type, Use Cutting Tap		5/32"	Max.
Brazing — With Use of Twin Carbon Torch. Clamp torch cable ends into ground clamp and electrode holder.	CARBON SIZE		
Brazing, Light Sheet Metal	1/4"	3/32"	Min.— 40
Brazing, Medium Sheet Metal	5/16"	or	Min.— 50
Brazing, Heavy Sheet Metal, Cast Iron	3/8"	1/8"	Min.— 100
Heating, Melting, Bending, Shaping	1/2"		100 — 180

Fig. 4-1. Welding guide chart. (Courtesy Century Mfg. Co.)

The thickness of the metal to be welded determines the diameter of the welding rod and the amount of heat you will need. The welder will have an infinitely variable heat range or a stepped range of ampere ratings, such as 40, 60, 80, and 100 amps. The chart in Fig. 4-1 is useful, although not definitive. If holes burn in light metal, or if the bead is flat and porous with an undercut edge, as illustrated in Figs. 4-2 and 4-3, you are using too much heat. If the bead looks as if it is heavily built up and just lying on top of the work surface, as in Fig. 4-4, too little heat is the culprit—the heat setting is too low, the arc is too long, or you have worked too fast. Too little heat makes the arc hard to hold, difficult to strike, and welds the electrode to the work.

When the heat range is correct, the arc will be easily struck and will draw smoothly over the work surface. No ragged edges will form, and the puddle will be at least as deep as the thickness of the rod.

Striking the Arc

To start the weld, you must first learn how to strike an arc. Striking an arc is done in much the same manner as is striking a

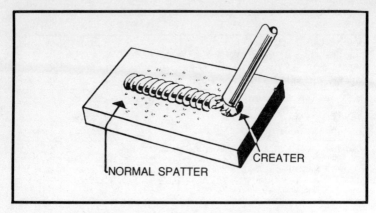

Fig. 4-2. Undercut bead. (Courtesy Century Mfg. Co.)

match: the tip of your electrode is scratched across the work surface near the area to be welded. Use a short stroke. The procedure must take place only when the welding helmet covers your eyes—certainly striking the arc, and maintaining it, in the near blind darkness of a welding helmet makes the chore harder for novice welders. Once struck it will give sufficient illumination. Viewing the arc without eye protection is equivalent to staring at the sun; look at

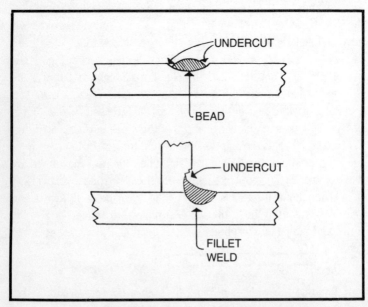

Fig. 4-3. Undercut fillet bead. (Courtesy Century Mfg. Co.)

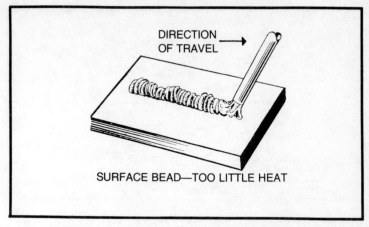

DIRECTION OF TRAVEL →

SURFACE BEAD—TOO LITTLE HEAT

Fig. 4-4. Surface bead. (Courtesy Century Mfg. Co.)

it long enough and you'll go blind. As you scratch the electrode, listen for a sputter. A fraction of a second later your arc will be struck.

Once you have struck your arc, raise the electrode, about an eighth-inch off the work surface. Some welding rods provide this gap automatically, but if the ones you are using don't, you will probably find this the single most difficult part of the job—it certainly is for me. If the rod is held too close to the work it will stick. If it is held too far away, you will lose your arc.

Should the electrode stick, it can be broken loose by rocking it back and forth.

Practice striking an arc with different metals and metal thicknesses. The reactions provided by different heat ranges, diffe-

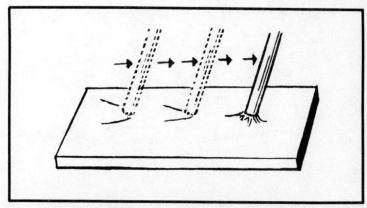

Fig. 4-5. Striking an arc. (Courtesy Century Mfg. Co.)

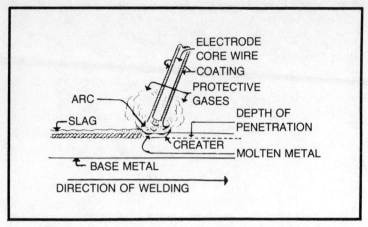

Fig. 4-6. Components of an arc. (Courtesy Century Mfg. Co.)

rent metals, and different size and composition welding rods will teach you far more about arc welding technique than you can learn from a book. Figure 4-6 shows the action that takes place as the arc is formed.

Once you have struck an arc, the electrode must be held still for an instant, but only an instant. This helps form the correct depth and size puddle for a strong bead, but too long a pause will burn a hole through the metal. The electrode is held at an angle to the work. You must also remember to continually keep moving the electrode closer to the work surface. Otherwise, you will lose the arc as the electrode is consumed. The best way to maintain the one-eighth inch distance for the arc, and to make certain your speed across the work surface

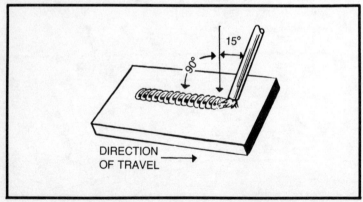

Fig. 4-7. Electrode angles when laying a bead (Courtesy Century Mfg. Co.)

is correct, is to keep an eye on the molten pool of metal that forms just behind the arc. Figure 4-7 shows direction and angle of travel along with a well formed bead.

Bead Formation

Several types of beads are used. The simplest is the stringer, or straight bead, which is laid in one continuous pass (Fig. 4-8). No movements to the side are made when a stringer bead is run. The electrode should be tipped back 15° in the direction of travel. The arc will throw the pool of molten metal away from the electrode which aids penetration of the base metal. Practice the straight bead until your welds are consistent and regular. The bead will, of course, be rippled, but the ripples should be smooth surfaced, blending gently into each other.

The weave bead is used to deposit metal over a wider, more open, joint than is the stringer bead, making a stronger fusion joint because of the increased metal buildup (Fig. 4-9). Weave beads are accomplished by moving the electrode from side to side with a slight hesitation at each edge.

OXY-ACETYLENE WELDING

Although there is similarity between arc and gas welding, there are enough differences to force us to practice each style separately.

Safety Precautions

Oxy-acetylene welding has certain hazards associated with it. The most obvious dangers are underscored here:

- Make sure all fittings are tight. Test for leaks with a solution of Ivory soap and warm water. A leak will show as bubbles.

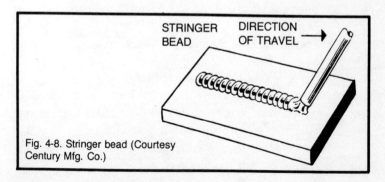

Fig. 4-8. Stringer bead (Courtesy Century Mfg. Co.)

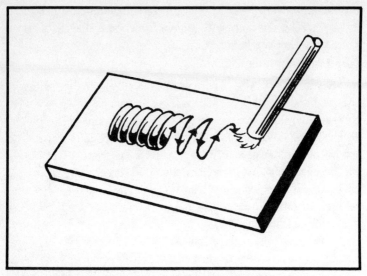

Fig. 4-9. Weave bead. (Courtesy Century Mfg. Co.)

- Don't force threaded fittings.
- Don't force the cylinder, regulator, or torch valves with a wrench. If the handle won't open or close the valve, there is something wrong and a repairman should check the equipment.
- Don't abuse the cylinders.
- Keep the acetylene cylinder upright, with the valve on top.
- Keep the acetylene-cylinder key on the valve stem to provide quick shutoff in an emergency.
- If the acetylene cylinder develops a leak, immediately move it outside into the open air and away from fires and open lights.
- Keep acetylene line pressure below 15 pounds per square inch (psi).
- Protect the hose from tangles, kinks, cuts, and being run over.
- Keep clear of spatters and hot slag.
- Make certain the hoses never come in contact with oil or grease. Petroleum products rot rubber and are an extreme hazard when combined with oxygen.
- Never oil the regulator. Oxygen will almost always start a flash fire when it contacts oil or grease.

- Make sure the space in which you are working is adequately ventilated. Welding fumes are health hazards.
- Do not weld near flammable materials.
- Wear safety goggles when cleaning work surfaces.
- Keep your hands clear of heated surfaces.
- Wear protective gear.

Protective Gear

People using oxy-acetylene and other gas welding equipment are seldom seen wearing full-face shields, as arc welders must. The full-face shield is still to be recommended for welding and brazing, and must be worn when cutting. For eye protection, use lens No. 4 for brazing and cutting, No. 5 for welding light-gauge sheet, and No. 6 for welding 1/8 to 1/2-inch steel plate.

Wear gloves and a longsleeved shirt. The shirt should be made of an organic fiber. As mentioned in an earlier section, man-made fibers increase the odds of splatter burns.

Hook Up

Your tanks are filled and ready; your hoses are laid out and ready to check. Move down the entire length of the hoses, from cylinder to torch tip, checking fittings. Make sure no dirt, especially grease or oil, is present. Dirt can block the seating of the fittings, while grease or oil can burst into flame in the presence of oxygen. Either situation is dangerous. Hose and fitting installation is simple for the reasons outlined in the previous chapter: Oxygen and acetylene fittings are incompatible and would have to be coupled by force.

Flame Temperatures

The neutral flame—the type used for most welding—has a temperature of about 5800°F (Fig. 4-10). Two other oxy-

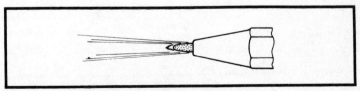

Fig. 4-10. Neutral flames. (Courtesy Turner Co., Div. of Olin Corp.)

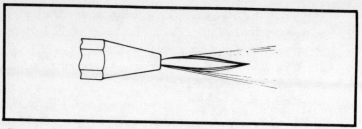

Fig. 4-11. Carburizing (fuel-rich) flame. (Courtesy Turner Co., Div. of Olin Corp.)

acetylene flames are familiar to welders. The carbonizing or reducing flame has a temperature of about 300° F less than a neutral flame, and should never be applied to ferrous metals (Fig. 4-11). The oxidizing flame, caused by an excess of oxygen (as the reducing flame is caused by an excess of acetylene), has a temperature of about 6000°F (Fig. 4-12). As you can see, oxyacetylene flames, while the hottest of all gas welding flames, are cooler than an electric arc.

Welding with Gas

Following the manufacturer's instructions to the letter, adjust the torch to give a neutral flame. A tack weld is a good starting point because of the relative ease with which it is made, and it is a very handy technique for later use. Tack welds can hold body panels while they are being seam welded. Tack welds are very handy for parts whose final configuration may have to be changed since the corrections can be made by breaking a few small, uncomplicated, and quickly remade welds.

Using sheet metal about the thickness of body panels (1/32 inch), lay two pieces side by side on a fireproof surface. Firebrick used in fireplaces is very handy for this work, and safer than asbestos board. Light up the torch and pull your welding goggles over your eyes.

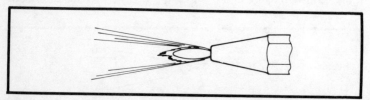

Fig. 4-12. Oxidizing (oxygen-rich) flame. (Courtesy Turner Co., Div. of Olin Corp.)

Adjust for a neutral flame and balance the torch in your hand.

After running the flame over the work surface a few times to warm things up, hold the flame close to the metal until the steel begins to melt and run together. As soon as the puddle forms and starts to flow, raise the torch. Otherwise you will burn through the thin metal. Warm the panels a bit longer by passing the flame over them several more times to prevent warping. That's your basic tack weld.

Using the same sheet metal panels, select a welding rod compatible with the material, and decide which of two gas-welding techniques to practice first. The forehand techniques require the tip of the torch to follow the welding rod; the backhand technique requires the tip of the torch to lead the rod.

Forehand welding may be done with a simple zigzag motion across the bead, or more complex circular movement (Fig. 4-13). These movements make the forehand method slightly harder to learn than the backhand method.

The backhand method requires no fancy tip movements, although the welding rod may be moved in circles or in arcs if desired. Backhand welding results in smaller, smoother puddles for the novice, providing cleaner and stronger welds.

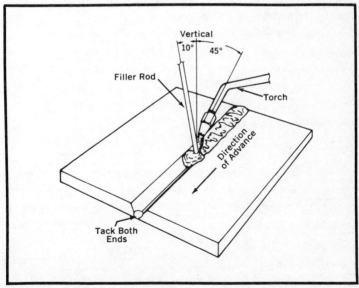

Fig. 4-13. Forehand welding. (Courtesy Turner Co., Div. of Olin Corp.)

The tip of the welding rod is melted by keeping it below the surface of the puddle. The rod should never come into contact with the inner cone of the torch flame, and the filler metal from the rod should never be allowed to simply drip into the puddle.

The practice panel is ready to be joined with a running bead. If the metal has not been tack welded already, it must be now.

Using—if you are like most people—the backhand method, apply heat to the end of the panel at the point where you wish to start the bead. Hold the torch with a loose, relaxed grip. Using the correct diameter welding rod—1/16 inch would be appropriate for this thickness of sheet metal—add rod to the puddle. Build the puddle to about half the diameter of the rod above the working surface. Keep the rod immersed in the puddle and the torch flame moving ahead of the rod.

Check the puddle appearance. If a white scum forms on the surface, you have an oxidizing flame and need to cut the oxygen back to return to a neutral flame.

Practice this type of simple weld until you are able to consistently produce smooth, even beads, similar in appearance to those you would want from an arc welder. Move to thicker metals for practice with a variety of rod and heat requirements. The same torch motions are used with thicker metal, but unless a larger tip is used, the rate of advance will be slower.

Heavy steel plates, such as those used in automobile frames, require edge beveling, and are really beyond the scope of this book. Those readers who are interested in developing welding skills should search out an adult education class on the subject. Welding is complex and seldom does a nonprofessional have much skill in more than a single aspect of the craft.

BRAZING BASICS

Many bodywork repairs are brazed. Brazing is called "welding" by those who do it, though most of them know better. Their reasoning runs something like: "Well, ol' Joe ain't gonna know the difference, and I don't feel up to explaining the reasons brazing can be better than welding for sheet metal."

Those reasons for the superiority of brazing certainly do exist. First, brazing is faster than fusion welding. Second, the heat required to braze is less than that needed to weld, cutting down on panel warp. Third, because it is faster and tends to do less violence to the work surface, brazing is cheaper than welding. Fourth, brazing can be used to join dissimilar metals, while fusion welding cannot. Extreme bead strength is not needed for most repair jobs and a braze is adequate.

Brazing is a gas technique and oxy-acetylene or oxy-propane equipment can be used, often without making a tip change. Most brazing rods used on automobile bodies are made from brass. Other rods—aluminum-silicon, copper, nickel-chromium, and magnesium—are sometimes used on special jobs. A carbon arc torch can be used with an arc welder for brazing. Carbon arc torches are harder to control than gas torches.

Flux is as essential to brazing as is a clean surface on both sides of the seam.

Copper-Alloy Brazing Techniques

Melting points for copper-alloy rods vary from about 1300°F to as high as 1850°F. Most are in the 1600°F range, with flow points—the temperature at which the rod becomes liquid—ranging from 10°F to 330°F above melting point. A wide spread between melting and flow points is a hindrance. It would help to start with a close spread, provided by 60/40 such as copper-zinc alloy (60% copper and 40% zinc). This alloy melts at 1650°F and flows freely at 1660°F.

Brazing demands careful edge and surface preparation. The panels to be joined are aligned and clamped. Tack welds or tack brazes can be made to assure alignment.

The panels should be preheated to reduce expansion and contraction stresses. A slight oxidizing flame—one that can be recognized by a small flame envelope and a pointed, white cone, is recommended by most experts. Figure 4-14 shows the flame adjustment for the Solidox torch, a very handy brazing tool. The oxidizing flame burns out some of the surface impurities always present in cast iron. These impurities would weaken the brazed joint. Use the same torch techniques as for fusion welding, with preference to the backhand method of torch manipulation.

Flux

Dry or paste fluxes are favored for brazing. The rod is heated and then dipped into the flux continaer.

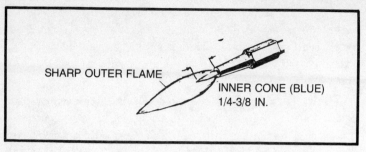

SHARP OUTER FLAME

INNER CONE (BLUE)
1/4-3/8 IN.

Fig. 4-14. Basic flame pattern for Solidox torches.

Care should be used around brazing (and welding) fluxes since these compounds often contain fluorides and other unfriendly elements that irritate the throat, nose, and eyes as well as the lungs.

While fluxes will float off many impurities from the surface of the metal being joined, they will not affect grease, oil, and grit. Mechanical means must be used for this job (soap, water, and, in extreme cases, a wire brush or power grinder).

Soldering And Soldering Tools

5

While soldering may seem an unnecessary skill for auto body repair, you will have occasion to use it. Certain lead-based solders are very handy for filling in low spots, filling small body holes, and seams. Solder makes a stronger, more flexible repair than does plastic filler. You will have to remove, move, or replace wiring, wiring terminals, and other electrical components. While solderless connections have become popular in recent years, no connection is as inexpensive to make or as reliable as a soldered joint.

Soldering is similar to brazing in principle, although soldered joints are weaker than brazed joints, and the temperatures used to make soldered joints are lower. All solders melt at temperatures below 800°F, while brazing rod melts at temperatures above 800°F. Temperatures between 500°F and 800°F are adequate for most soft solders; indeed, higher temperatures are often harmful.

TOOLS AND SUPPLIES

The solders that interest us here are tin-lead compounds, which, depending on the amount of each metal in the alloy, are known as tin or lead solders.

An oxy-acetylene torch is too much for soldering by a novice, who will find it difficult to control the heat. Propane torches, details of which are shown in Figs. 5-1, 5-2, and 5-3, are the best choice for

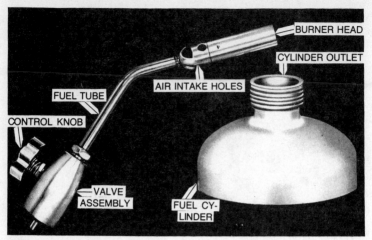

Fig. 5-1. Propane torch assembly showing the external parts. (Courtesy Turner Co., Div. of Olin Corp.)

soldering—at least insofar as the home craftsman is concerned. Professionals prefer to use oxy-acetylene torches with special tips for soft soldering.

A soldering iron can be used as shown in Fig. 5-4, when small areas must be soldered although a propane torch is necessary when filling dents and wide seams. A soldering gun is the most appropriate tool for automotive wiring, though you will need a fairly large one.

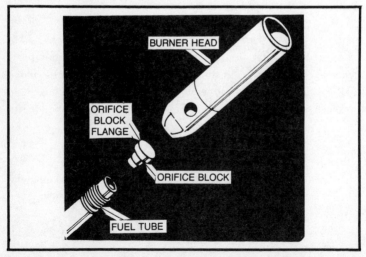

Fig. 5-2. Propane torch tip assembly. (Courtesy Turner Co., Div. of Olin Corp.)

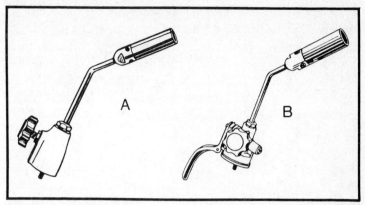

Fig. 5-3. The standard torch must be lighted each time (view A); the Turner instant-flame torch has a pilot.

The smallest gun with utility around an automobile draws 200 watts; the preference goes to those with ratings of 225 watts and more. A dual-range gun will allow you to solder delicate wiring as well as moderately heavy cable.

PREPARATION

Soldering depends upon surface cleanliness. Because the low temperatures used during soldering operations can not burn off

Fig. 5-4. Small holes and dents can sometimes be filled with solder.

impurities, cleanliness is even more important than it is in welding or brazing. The surface should first be rough cleaned with a file or grinder to remove paint and rust. Polish the surface with a fine grade of steel wool. Then flush off any traces of grease or oil with solvent. Remove the solvent with water and apply soldering flux to remove surface oxidation. Flux forms a thin film over the sheet metal, preventing contact with the surrounding air and the formation of more oxides.

For electrical work, noncorrosive rosin flux is recommended, while for body filling, a corrosive, or acid, flux should be used because of its stronger action. When corrosive fluxes are used, you must scrub all traces of the flux from the surface metal as soon as the solder has set. If the excess is not removed, the surface surrounding the soldered area will quickly corrode.

Soldering iron and gun tips must be cleaned and tinned. A wire brush, of relatively fine wire size, is used to clean the tip, and then the iron is heated (this procedure is changed slightly with soldering guns, for their more delicate tips do not take kindly to a wire brush). Use crocus or emery cloth instead. Sprinkle some flux on the iron or gun tip, and rub the hot tip with solder. Tinning is complete when a thin coat of solder adheres to the tip.

Open-flame soldering does not, of course, involve tinning. However, solid soldering tips are available for some torches and these tips must be cleaned and tinned.

BODY SOLDERING

For body soldering, or leading in, the area to be filled is cleaned as discussed above. Bar lead or solder is then melted with a propane torch (a large soldering iron can be used, but the torch is easier to control for most people). As the solder melts it is spread over the area to be filled with a body paddle. If the surface is properly prepared, including fluxing and tinning, the bond between the lead and sheet metal will be very strong. As described here, leading in is best used for filling small dents or holes where chrome moldings or decorations have been removed and discarded. See Chapter 9 for more details on large-surface body leading.

As the solder is being worked, care must be taken to see that it stays plastic, but without reaching the molten state. If the solder melts, it will flow off vertical surfaces.

Body lead is built up until it is a fraction of an inch or so higher than the surrounding metal to allow for filing and sanding.

A body file can be used for finish shaping, but a general-duty No. 24 open-coat sanding disc will do a quicker and neater job on small areas (Fig. 5-5).

Fig. 5-5. Small grinders are a necessity in bodywork.

If you need to solder aluminum, your best bet is to use a solder that has a self-contained flux and follow the manufacturer's instructions to the letter. Aluminum bodies are difficult to solder for two reasons. First, aluminum conducts heat away from the work area very rapidly; second, aluminum surfaces oxidize quickly, and the solder may not adhere. In most cases, aluminum is better repaired by welding (a technique for experts) or by the use of special plastic body fillers (an expedient that will not suit the person with a custom-bodied sports car, I'm afraid).

Of course, once the surface of the aluminum is tinned, few problems remain, for the aluminum is no longer exposed to the oxidizing effects of the open air, and soldering can then easily take place, just as it would with any other body panel. It's the tinning that drives you up the wall.

WIRING

When a panel is badly damaged or totaled, and the wiring in that panel cannot be saved, soldering will allow you to add only the wire necessary to the circuits involved. In other words, you can splice into the feed circuit without going back to the terminal blocks. At today's copper prices, any savings in this area are appreciated.

Assuming that you have two wires to splice, strip the insulation about 1 inch back from the ends of the wires. Since automotive wiring is stranded, the ends should be twisted together to prevent separation. It is always good practice to twist the wires together for mechanical strength.

Shrink-fit tubing, available at electronics supply houses, is an ideal insulation. Use the soldering iron or gun to heat the wires and then hold rosin-core solder to the hot wires until the solder flows into the strands. Remove the heat source as soon as enough solder has flowed to fill in the strands as shown in Fig. 5-6, but before any buildup forms on the outside of the connection. Do not move the joint until the solder has set, or you will have what is known as a cold joint, a point of high resistance in the circuit and a hard-to-trace source of trouble.

Once the solder has set—to be safe give it a couple of minutes—slip the shrink-fit tubing over the joint and slowly move a match around the tubing. It will shrink to provide a nearly invisible insulated joint. Voila! Completed wiring, a good circuit, fully insulated.

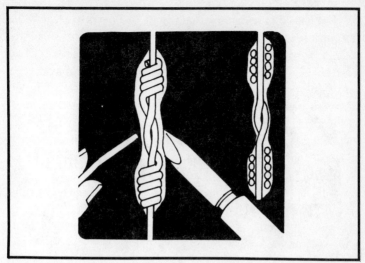

Fig. 5-6. Soldering wire can be done with a torch and soldering tip. (Courtesy Turner Co., Div. of Olin Corp.)

Other methods of insulation are possible. Shrink-fit tape is available, which works the same way but is intended for larger connections than those covered by available tubing sizes. Then there is, for those who want a completely weatherproof seal, the option of coating the bare connection with GE's RTV silicone sealant (or some other brand, if you prefer) and wrapping the connection with plastic electrician's tape.

Panel Replacement

There comes a time when patching, filling, and straightening are useless. When a panel is severely rusted or crumpled, it must be replaced.

PARTS SOURCES

Fortunately most parts you might wish to replace on cars up to seven or eight years old are available from new car dealers. Parts for these same cars, as well as older models, can be found at wrecking yards, often as complete units that need only a coat of paint to make them match the original finish.

Economic considerations determine whether you buy a replacement part or refinish the old one. If a fender is going to require $10 worth of heat and lead, plus four hours of work to refinish, there is not much point is spending $100 or more for a new one. But if the fender is rusted or crumpled to the extent that it must be welded, dinged out, leaded, and then painted, work that requires $50 or more in materials and several days' labor, then the economics of the situation calls for replacement.

In many cases, parts no longer produced by Detroit can be bought from other suppliers, companies that have made molds from the original parts and sell reproductions. These parts usually cost more than originals, but with no originals available, there is no choice. Builders of street rods have gone down this road: Twenty years ago, grille shells for 1932 Fords started to become scarce. If a metal shell were found today, the price would be astronomical, but several companies sell fiberglass reproductions at prices that are quite reasonable in comparison.

It is also possible to lighten a car by using glass and plastic body parts, but care must be used in the selection. Most companies producing this sort of material offer two grades, or weights, one classified as street weight (sometimes close to the weight of the original metal component) and one classified as racing weight (very much lighter than the original pieces). For example, Anderson Industries, Inc., (5625 Furnace Avenue, Elkridge, Maryland 21227) offers every part they sell in two weights, but racing weight is strictly for competition. While it may sound odd that racing cars are able to use lighter body components than street machines, few racing cars are exposed to the sort of day in, day out pounding that a passenger car must take.

Prices will certainly change, but a few examples can give you an idea of the cost of fiberglass components. Anderson Industries asks $115 (plus shipping) for a 1974 Camaro hood; the grille panel for the Rallye Sport goes for $150. Fenders cost $115.

It pays to check several wrecking yards. Not only is this often a way to save money, it can just as frequently be a way to save time. Many automobile dealers do not carry extensive lines of body panels, preferring to order them as needed. The result is that it may take you five or six weeks to get the new part. In addition most wrecking yards have reference books that tell what panel from a particular year will fit other years of the same make. It is a great timesaver to be able to replace a fender on a 1975 car with one from a 1974 or a 1976 model, as there are times when an appropriate wreck is not available. I've seen the day, looking for front-end parts, when it seemed as if every car we looked at had had major damage to the very parts needed.

PANEL INSTALLATION

Front-fender panels are easy to remove and replace, since the fenders are bolted on (with an occasional spot weld). The only difficulty—and it is not a major one—is removing rusted bolts. If penetrating oil does not work, simply twist the bolt off with a wrench or Vise-Grips. Once the fender is removed, carefully drill out the bolt and replace it with a new one.

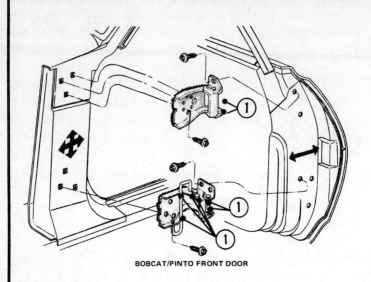

BOBCAT/PINTO FRONT DOOR

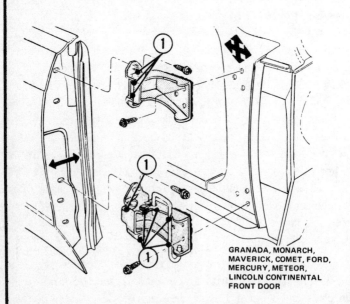

GRANADA, MONARCH,
MAVERICK, COMET, FORD,
MERCURY, METEOR,
LINCOLN CONTINENTAL
FRONT DOOR

Fig. 6-1. Ford door-hinge adjustment and lubrication points—except Torino, Elite, Montego, Thunderbird, and Continental Mark IV.

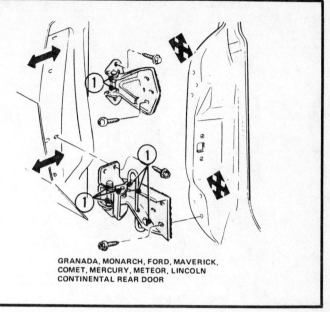

GRANADA, MONARCH, FORD, MAVERICK,
COMET, MERCURY, METEOR, LINCOLN
CONTINENTAL REAR DOOR

Large panels require serious surgery to remove and must be welded or brazed into place. While an expert bodyworker can cut a panel out with a torch, the novice should invest in a nibbler, a tool that does a fairly good job of cutting sheet metal without distorting the edges. You're asking for trouble if you use a saber saw. The new panel is cut to exactly match the hole left by the old one and welded or tack brazed. The open seams between the welds are easy enough to fill.

Small panels are less subject to heat distortion and are often stressed to bear some of the body load. These panels are fusion welded, as described in Chapter 4.

DOORS

One of the routine bodywork jobs is to realign a sagging door. Unless there has been serious frame damage, the door hinges will provide sufficient adjustment to correct the problem. With the exception of the welded hinges on the Vega, mounting holes in the door or post side of the hinges are elongated. Figures 6-1 and 6-2 show Ford doors' lubrication and adjustment points. Figure 6-3 shows Chrysler-Plymouth adjustments and Fig. 6-4 illustrates the tool Chrysler recommends for hinge adjustments.

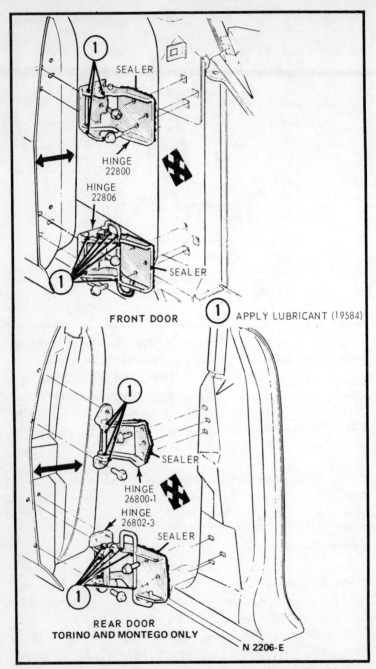

Fig. 6-2. Ford hinge adjustment and lubrication points—Torino, Elite, Montego, Cougar, Thunderbird, and Continental Mark IV.

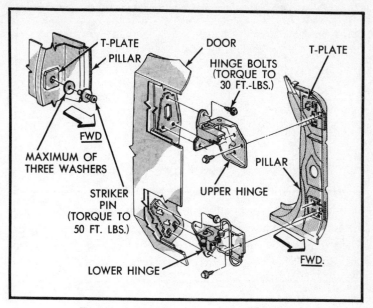

Fig. 6-3. Chrysler front-door hinges and striker.

The latch striker, or striker pin, as shown in Fig. 6-5, can also be adjusted, and will often have to be if major hinge adjustments are made. It is possible to cover up problems with hinge alignment by adjusting the striker pin so that it will catch and hold. Don't. Make corrections at the hinge until the door fits squarely. Loosen the hinge bolts enough to allow movement when a padded pry bar is used for leverage. Tighten the hinge bolts after each adjustment. If there is bind or interference with other body panels, estimate the distance and direction the door must be moved, back off the bolts, and readjust. As necessary, adjust the door-latch striker.

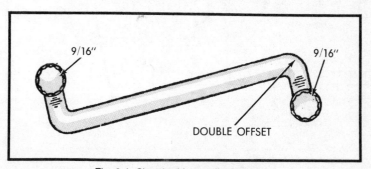

Fig. 6-4. Chrysler hinge-adjustment tool.

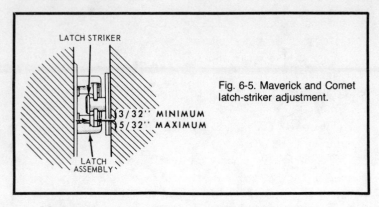

Fig. 6-5. Maverick and Comet latch-striker adjustment.

LATCH STRIKER

3/32" MINIMUM
5/32" MAXIMUM

LATCH ASSEMBLY

Most latch strikers offer lateral and vertical adjustment, often by means of shims (available from dealers.) Ford recommends checking the fit by first wiping the old grease from the latch jaws and the striker. Then coat the striker with dark grease. As the door is

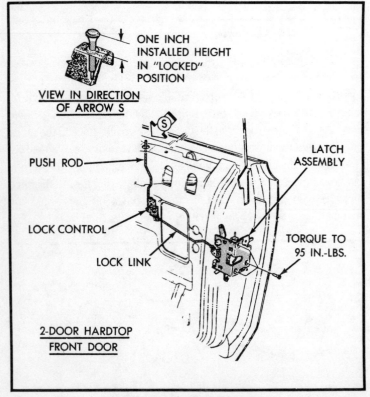

ONE INCH
INSTALLED HEIGHT
IN "LOCKED"
POSITION

VIEW IN DIRECTION
OF ARROW S

PUSH ROD

LOCK CONTROL

LOCK LINK

LATCH ASSEMBLY

TORQUE TO
95 IN.-LBS.

2-DOOR HARDTOP
FRONT DOOR

Fig. 6-6. Chrysler latch pushrod.

closed and opened, the pattern formed by the dark grease will provide you with enough information to make the adjustment.

Figure 6-6 shows how the latch push-rod is attached to the door latch on Chrysler front-door assembly. Removal and reinstallation is straightforward and is done through the access holes shown in the illustration.

Figures 6-7 and 6-8 show the lock pushbutton arrangement on Ford front doors.

These illustrations are typical, but can not do justice to the complexity of the subject—it pays to keep track of what you are doing. Study the joints as you disassemble the unit.

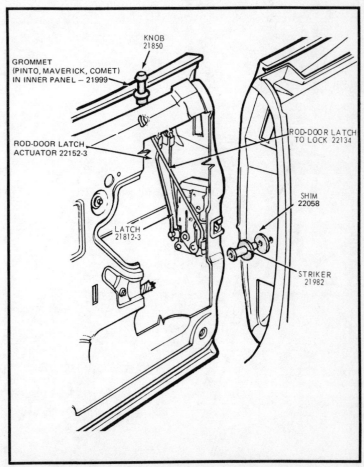

Fig. 6-7. Typical Ford latch- and striker-adjustment points.

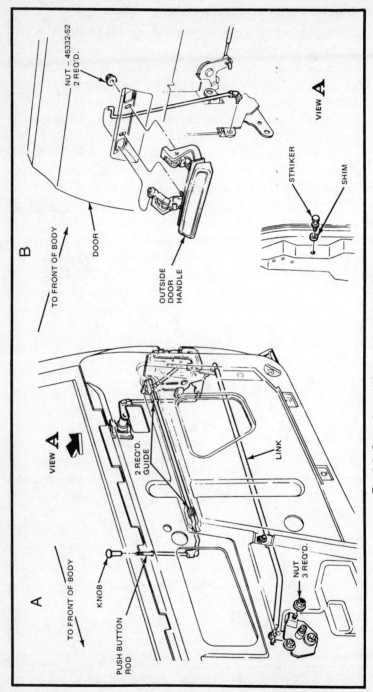

Fig. 6-8. Granada and Monarch front-door latch mechanisms.

B

NUT – 45332-S2
2 REQ'D.

DOOR

TO FRONT OF BODY

OUTSIDE
DOOR
HANDLE

VIEW **A**

STRIKER

SHIM

VIEW **A**

A

TO FRONT OF BODY

KNOB

PUSH BUTTON
ROD

2 REQ'D.
GUIDE

LINK

NUT
3 REQ'D.

HOODS

Hoods are frequent replacement items because of accident damage. A hood is more difficult for the inexperienced person to align than is a door, though it needn't be. The difficulty is in supporting the mass of metal above one's head while attempting to make attachments and adjustments.

Two people are needed to remove a hood on a large American car. Cover the cowl and fenders with blankets. Prop the hood full open and place a block of wood between it and the cowl. The wood will protect the windshield. Scribe a mark around the hood hinges as an installation guide. Hood hinge torsion bars must be disconnected and removed on Chrysler products (Fig. 6-9). Others are released by removing the hinge bolts (Fig. 6-10). Take care to keep the hood from slipping when the bolts are removed—which is the major reason for a second person.

Hood latch and cable removal is sometimes necessary. Figure 6-11 provides a detailed look at a remote-control release for Chrysler products, while Fig. 6-12 does the same for Ford compacts.

Installation of the hood requires an assistant who maintains the hood's position while the bolts are loosely run in. Use the scribed marks as a reference. On Chrysler products, the torsion bars are installed while the bolts are still loose. The retaining-bracket nuts must be torqued 95 inch-pounds, and the bars are then positioned in the slider ramps. Refer to Fig. 6-9 for details. Bring the attachment-plate bolts up snug and lower the hood slowly and gently for an alignment check.

Elongated holes in the hinges allow fore, aft, and lateral movements. Make the cowl-to-hood adjustment first. Then try for equal spacing on each side of the hood at the fenders.

If necessary, the latch and safety catch can be adjusted. The fit should be checked whenever a hood is removed, even though the same hood is reinstalled. The latch can be moved from side to side and (on most vehicles) the striker adjusts vertically.

TRUNK LIDS

Trunk-lid replacement is simpler than hood replacement because the lid weighs less. Still, an assistant is helpful, particularly on large cars. Remove the hinge bolts at the lid (Figs. 6-13 and 6-14).

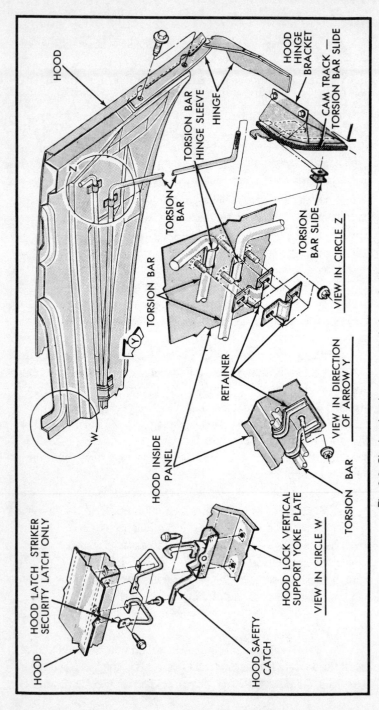

Fig. 6-9. Chrysler hoods are counterbalanced with torsion bars.

HOOD

HOOD

TORSION BAR

TORSION BAR HINGE SLEEVE
HINGE

TORSION BAR

HOOD HINGE BRACKET

CAM TRACK — TORSION BAR SLIDE

TORSION BAR SLIDE

VIEW IN CIRCLE Z

HOOD INSIDE PANEL

RETAINER

VIEW IN DIRECTION OF ARROW Y

TORSION BAR

HOOD LATCH STRIKER
SECURITY LATCH ONLY

HOOD

HOOD LOCK VERTICAL SUPPORT YOKE PLATE

VIEW IN CIRCLE W

HOOD SAFETY CATCH

As you undo the bolts, your helper will steady the lid. It's a good idea to cover the rear fenders with blankets during removal and installation.

To replace, reverse the procedure, with your assistant supporting the lid so bolts can be inserted easily: Paint scores under the bolts serve as guides for the initial adjustment.

TAILGATES

Station-wagon tailgates come in a multitude of styles, from side swinging to down swinging to dual swinging to manual window to power window to power lock to...a lot of different things. Figure 6-15 shows the basic single-action tailgate assembly. Fig. 6-16 illustrates a current Chrysler application.

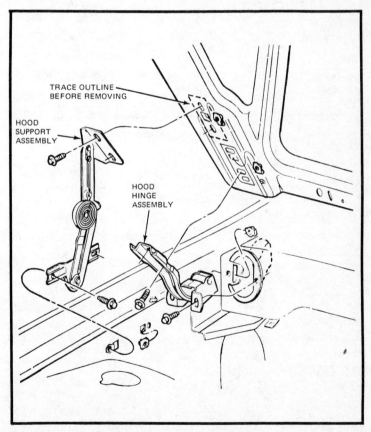

Fig. 6-10. Granada and Monarch hoods are supported on conventional springs.

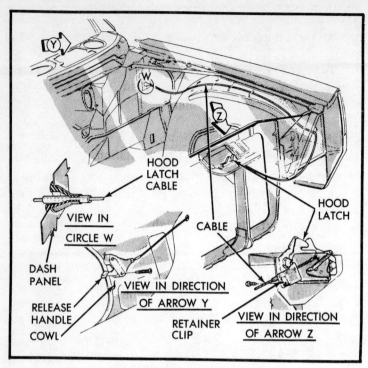

Fig. 6-11. Chrysler control-cable release.

I will cover removal, installation, and adjustment of the Chrysler model, since it is more complex. The same techniques can be adapted to other makes and models.

Remove the interior trim panel and disconnect the electrical leads. Remove the check arm (gate swing limiter) and torsion bar guide, from the pillar plates.

Support the tailgate on jackstands, with padding on their tops to prevent damage. Loosen the hinge pivot pins. If the same tailgate is to be reinstalled, scribe an outline of the hinge-plate on the pillar post. Remove the hinge plate bolts from the pillar post, and slide the hinge plate and torsion bar in through the bar guide (toward the center of the tailgate). Lower the tailgate off the car.

To install, push the torsion bar and hinge plates in toward the center of the tailgate. Then slip the plates into the lower body opening, and attach the hinge plate bolts to the pillar posts (with the hinge plates located in the marked position, if this is the original tailgate). Tighten the bolts enough to hold the tailgate in position and

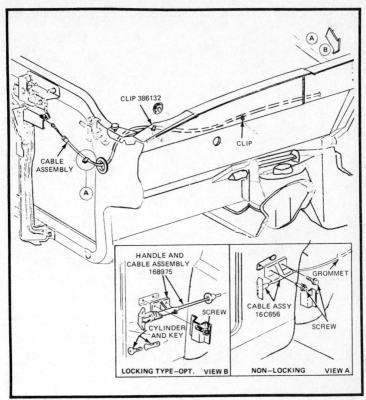

Fig. 6-12. Control cable release—Mustang, Granada, Monarch, Pinto, and Bobcat.

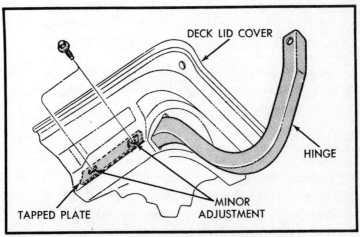

Fig. 6-13. Chrysler trunk-lid hinges mount in sliders.

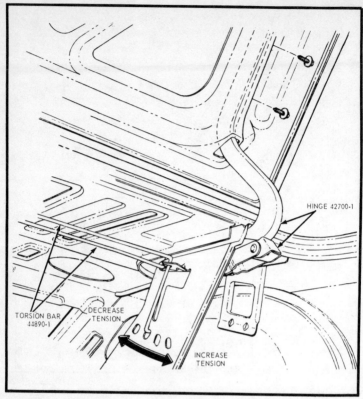

Fig. 6-14. Some Ford trunk lids are swung on adjustable torsion bars.

check the alignment. Center the tailgate in its opening, and attach the torsion-bar bracket to the pillar post. Open the tailgate and tighten the locking screws on the hinge-pivot pin. Connect the electrical leads.

If the window-lift mechanism has been disturbed, slowly raise the window, checking the alignment of the glass in its channels. This is one spot a poor fit can mean breakage.

RADIATOR SUPPORTS

Radiator-yoke supports are vulnerable to collision damage, and may require replacement. First, drain the radiator and disconnect the hoses. Remove the shroud and the radiator-mounting bolts and lift the radiator out. Depending upon the model, the hood striker bar, horn, and headlamp wiring may also have to be removed. There are wheelhouse-to-yoke supporting screws under the front fenders on many cars. These must be removed, and then the screws attaching the frame to the yoke can be removed. The assembly, shown in Fig. 6-17, will then lift out.

Installation of new parts is the reverse of the removal procedure. Screws should be run up lightly before tightening any. Tighten the screws progressively, a few turns at a time.

BUMPERS

On older cars, bumper replacement is simple. Just unbolt the old part, toss it away, line up the new part with the braces, and bolt it on. Unfortunately, this convenience has been sacrificed to meet crashworthiness standards. Most modern cars have impact-absorbing bumpers that move inward during collision. The space between the bumper and chassis is covered by plastic panels known as bumper fillers or right shields.

If no metal beyond the bumper is bent, the job is fairly simple, though impact absorbers make things unwieldy since they are quite heavy. Parking-lamps must be disconnected on those models with lamps incorporated in the bumper. Details of current Chrysler front and rear bumpers are shown in Fig. 6-18, and a typical Ford front bumper in Fig. 6-19. In nearly all cases, removal is a simple unbolting job, with additional bolts for the impact-absorbing system, if the car has such a feature. Upon reassembly, the impact absorbers are installed first, then flexible filler inserts, and the bumper is lifted into place (you can use jack stands for supports if you are working alone) and bolted on. Check the bumper alignment along the right and left fenders, at the grille and rear deck, and align as required to get the spacing equal. Tighten all mounting nuts, and reconnect any wiring that was taken loose previously.

FENDERS

Figure 6-20 shows a typical fender assembly. To remove, disconnect the battery ground strap. Protect the leading edge of the front door and the cowl adjacent to the fender with masking tape.

Remove the front bumper, and disconnect the wiring to the lights. Remove the stud nuts or screws that hold the grille to the fender. Remove the nuts and screws securing the fender to the cowl, floor sill, wheelhouse (inner fender or splash shield), and

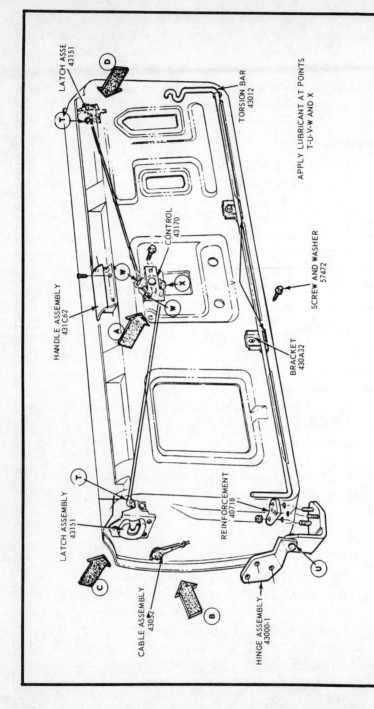

LATCH ASSE 43151

D

TORSION BAR 43012

APPLY LUBRICANT AT POINTS T-U-V-W AND X

CONTROL 43170

HANDLE ASSEMBLY 431C62

W

W

A

X

V

SCREW AND WASHER 57472

BRACKET 430A32

T

LATCH ASSEMBLY 43151

T

REINFORCEMENT 40718

C

CABLE ASSEMBLY 43052

B

HINGE ASSEMBLY 43000-1

U

78

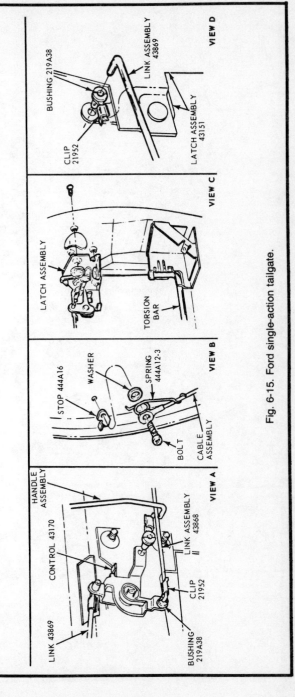

Fig. 6-15. Ford single-action tailgate.

79

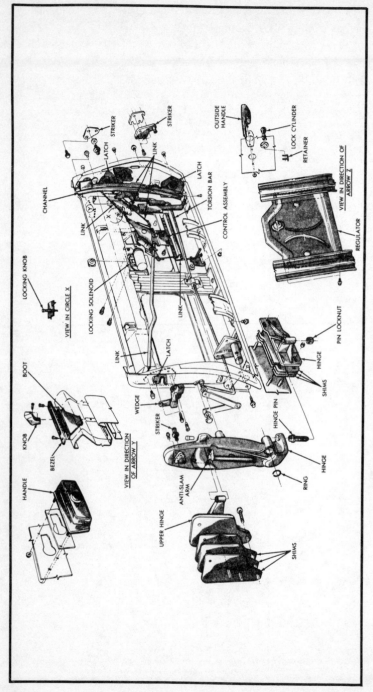

Fig. 6-16. Chrysler wagons are fitted with this rather imposing tailgate.

radiator yoke. Lift off the assembly and salvage any reusable parts such as trim molding, headlight shell, and so on.

The installation procedure depends in part upon whether the painting will be done with the fender on or off the car. It is wiser to spray the color coat after the fender is mounted; you may scratch the new finish as you install the fender. But if the fender has been painted, install the headlamps and decorative trim. If the fender has only been primed, this step is omitted for now. Carefully position the fender on the studs on the cowl side of the car, and line it up with the mounting holes in the radiator yoke. Install the mounting screws and retaining nuts. Check the fender alignment. The fender should be positioned to provide equal spacing at the cowl and at the front and top edges of the door. Alignment should also be checked at the bottom of the floor-sill panel, the front of the hood and the door.

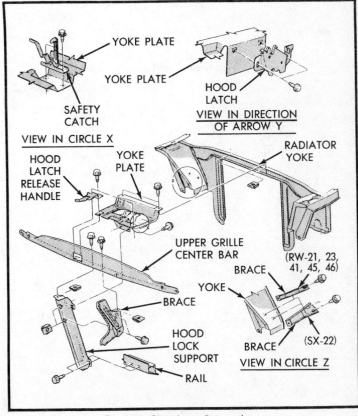

Fig. 6-17. Chrysler radiator yoke.

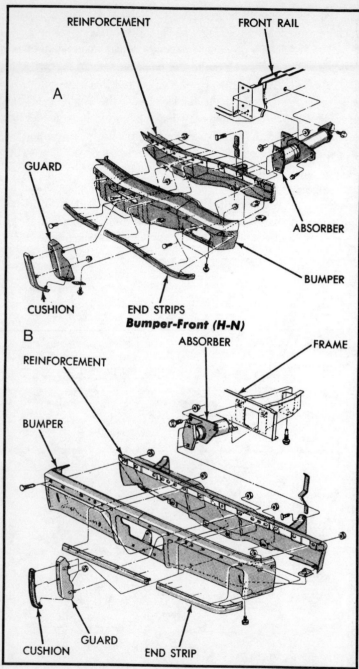

REINFORCEMENT FRONT RAIL

A

GUARD

CUSHION END STRIPS

ABSORBER

BUMPER

Bumper-Front (H-N)

B

REINFORCEMENT

BUMPER

ABSORBER FRAME

CUSHION GUARD END STRIP

Fig. 6-18. Chrysler front bumper (view A) and rear (view B).

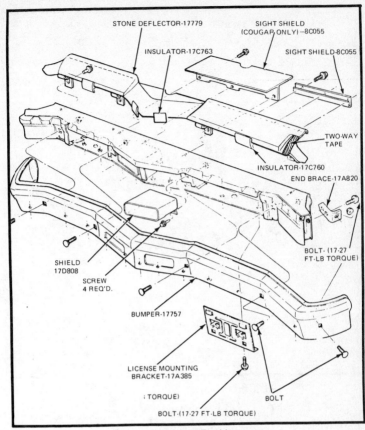

Fig. 6-19. Typical Ford bumper.

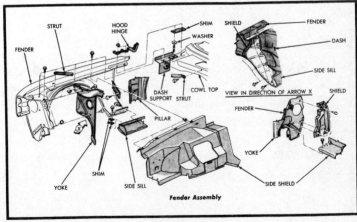

Fig. 6-20. Chrysler fender assembly.

83

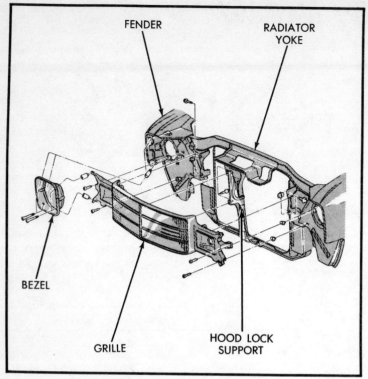

FENDER

RADIATOR YOKE

BEZEL

GRILLE

HOOD LOCK SUPPORT

Fig. 6-21. Chrysler grille assembly.

Once the fender is correctly aligned, tighten the nuts and screws progressively, making sure that the fender remains in alignment.

After the fender is secured, connect the wiring and install the grille fender nuts. Reconnect the ground strap.

GRILLES

A Chrysler grille assembly is shown in Fig. 6-21. The variations in grille design and mounting techniques are wide, and it is impossible to give step-by-step instructions here. Make sure that all nuts, bolts, and screws have been removed before attempting to pull out a grille section, for some of these fasteners are cleverly hidden. Do not pry on modern plastic grills any more than necessary. And under no circumstances apply heat.

Interior Trim, Carpeting and Headliners

A good indicator of the age of an automobile is the condition of the upholstery, rugs, trim panels, headliner and package tray. A few hours of work can refinish a shabby interior to an as-new condition.

This book is not the place to discuss automobile upholstery in detail, but it is possible to look at how replacement seat covers should be attached for best results, at how carpeting can be laid so that it stays down and lasts, and how new trim panels can easily be installed.

REARVIEW MIRRORS

Rearview mirrors are seldom thought of until they fog, or refuse to hold adjustment. Replacement, in every case, should be simple. Two methods of mounting the mirror are in use. Many are simply screwed to the front part of the headliner of the car. These are simplest: unscrew the old mirror, discard it, and screw in the new mirror.

Mirrors mounted on the windshield with a button, that is, a pad of cemented vinyl, are more difficult in that removal takes longer and care is needed in order not to damage the windshield. First, remove the mirror from the pad: It will be held on with a set screw. If the pad also needs to be replaced, use a grease pencil or a crayon to mark its location on the windshield, and then use an electric hair drier to soften the vinyl. Peel the vinyl from the windshield with a razor

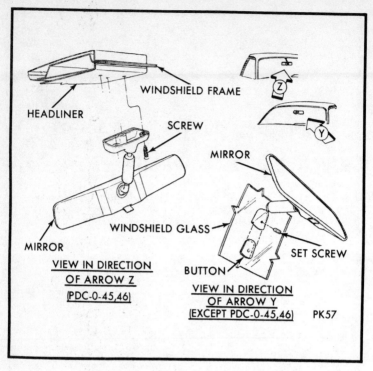

Fig. 7-1. Chrysler rearview-mirror installation.

blade. Exercise extreme care, for it is at this point that the windshield can be damaged. Next, completely clean the area where the new pad is to be installed (of course, do the cleaning on the inside of your grease-pencil markings). Chrysler recommends a mild cleansing powder on a pad saturated with alcohol. Then use fine sandpaper to abrade the bottom of the mounting pad.

A mounting kit is supplied with the new mounting pad. Thoroughly mix the accelerator, or catalyst, with the adhesive and apply a thin film to both surfaces.

Position the mounting pad with reference to your grease-pencil marks, press down hand, and hold for about 1 minute.

After the adhesive has had 5 or 10 minutes to cure, remove any excess squeezed out around the edges of the pad, with an alcohol dampened cloth. Slip the mirror into place on the mounting pad and tighten the set screw.

Figure 7-1 shows both types of installation for Chrysler products.

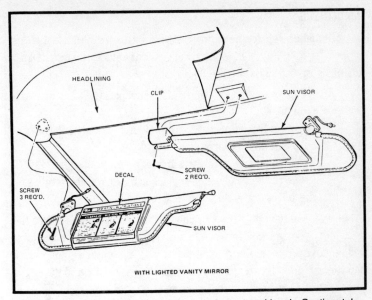

HEADLINING

CLIP

SUN VISOR

SCREW
2 REQ'D.

DECAL

SCREW
3 REQ'D.

SUN VISOR

WITH LIGHTED VANITY MIRROR

Fig. 7-2. This lighted visor is standard equipment on Lincoln Continentals.

SUN VISORS

Slip the old visors off and the new ones on. Some cars have fancier setups, with lighted vanity mirrors on the visor (Fig. 7-2). Figure 7-3 provides detailed closeups that show how to work on this particular frill.

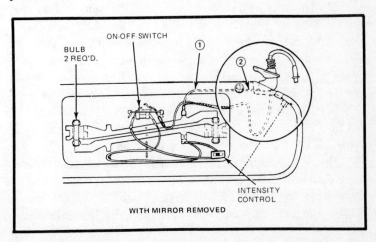

ON-OFF SWITCH

BULB
2 REQ'D.

① ②

INTENSITY
CONTROL

WITH MIRROR REMOVED

Fig. 7-3. The internals are accessible with the mirror removed. (Courtesy Ford Motor Co.)

HEADLINERS

Headliner replacement on some cars is more difficult than on others, for a variety of reasons: One reason is evident when looking at Ford's instructions for the Maverick:

1. Remove the right and left windshield wiper arm assemblies.
2. Remove the windshield and moldings by using the procedure outlined in Group 43.
3. Remove the weatherstrip from the glass opening.
4. Remove the rear window glass from the opening by using the procedures outlined in Group 43.

Once you have to remove major glass from a car to replace the headliner, you can look forward to some tense times. Glass removal will be covered in another chapter but is is a job that requires care and special tools. If care isn't exercised, the gasket around the edges of the glass may leak, or the glass may shatter.

The simplest way to find out whether or not you'll have to remove windshield and rear window is to ask the dealer. Don't try to stuff the edge in under the windshield gasket. It won't hold properly, and the new lining will sag badly in short order.

Headliner removal begins with the removal of the rear seat cushion, the dome light(s), sun visors, coat hooks, and any other accessories that mount through the surface of the liner.

The headliner is then peeled back from the cemented areas at the top of the windshield and rear window. A dull putty knife can be used to pull the fabric from the side-rail retainers. If the linen is to be reused, work it out of the retainers a few inches at a time.

The headliner is then slipped out from under the windshield garnish molding and from any fasteners in the rear-window area, together with the support, or listing, wires at the sides and rear. The headliner now should be free. Lay it aside and remove the remaining cement from above the rear window and windshield.

The new headliner should be laid face down on a clean surface, and the old liner laid on top of it for a pattern. Locate and mark areas for hole cutting: These include dome light cutouts, possible cutouts for sun visor mounts, possible cutouts for shoulder-harness mounts, and so on.

Locate the centerline of the windshield and rear-window openings. Simply measure the width and pick the center point, using chalk to mark the spots. Now locate and mark the centerline of the new headliner (just fold it down the middle and pull the edges up even). Make small X cuts in the centers of all spots where holes will have to be cut.

Insert the listing wires from the old liner into the appropriate spaces in the new liner. See Fig. 7-4 for details of a Chrysler headliner. You may want to install insulation between the roof and headliner, to cut down on noise and heat loss. Make sure the insulation will not interfere with the installation of the new headliner.

Center the headliner at the rear window opening and insert the rear listing wire into the retainer clips on the roof-rail extension. The rear listing wire is now hooked to its wire supports and the material is stretched just enough to remove all the wrinkles and bring it into front and rear alignment. The rest of the listing wires are placed into the roof's side-rail retainers, making sure the material remains wrinkle-free and aligned.

Now apply cement to the windshield header using the type recommended by the automaker, or any good contact cement. Position the headliner on the cemented area, starting from the centerline of the windshield.

With your dull putty knife, attach the liner to the barbs in the header area, allowing the material to stand clear of the tops of the windshield posts. Keep fabric seams straight and eliminate all wrinkles.

Cut holes for the sun-visor screws, making them slightly larger than the diameter of the screws. Install the sun visors and tuck in the material at the top of the windshield posts. If the rearview mirror is mounted through the headliner, cut holes for its mounting-bracket screws.

Now, install the headliner along the side rails of the roof, working a small section at a time. The dull putty knife is again used to install the headliner in the side-rail retainers.

Cement is now applied at the rear-window opening and around the quarter-panel area. Install the headliner, starting at the top center and working down and out toward the sides, keeping seams straight and making sure that no wrinkles are present.

Locate the areas for installation of coat hooks and the dome light. Any necessary holes should be cut and the trim mounted.

That will just about cover the installation of fabric headliners. One other type of headliner is used in some automobiles: Hardboard.

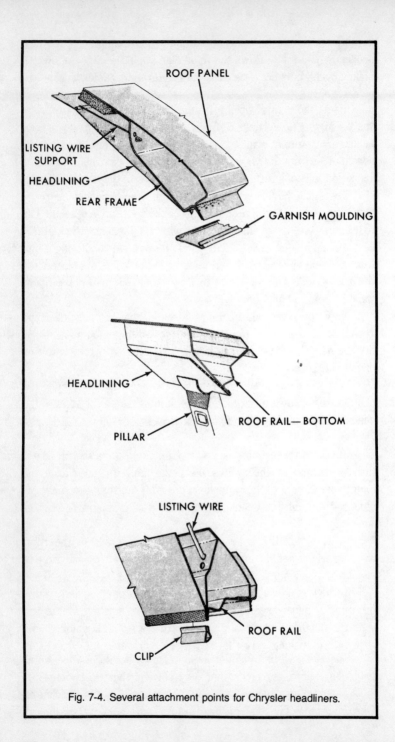

ROOF PANEL

LISTING WIRE
SUPPORT

HEADLINING

REAR FRAME

GARNISH MOULDING

HEADLINING

PILLAR

ROOF RAIL—BOTTOM

LISTING WIRE

ROOF RAIL

CLIP

Fig. 7-4. Several attachment points for Chrysler headliners.

In some ways, hardboard is easier to install than fabric since it will already be cut to size, with most accessory holes cut or punched. It's a matter of removing the old material, mounting the hardboard liner, and fitting the panels in the correct order. It is usually better to start at the rear of the top piece of hardboard liner and move forward and down from there. Figure 7-5 shows the stages of installation for hardboard headliners in Chrysler station wagons.

SEATBELTS

The writer is a firm believer in seatbelts for a very simple reason: Statistics prove that seatbelts and shoulder harnesses save lives.

Most people do not realize that care is needed to maintain the belts in working order, and too many of us overlook the belts when reupholstering or otherwise repairing the interior of an automobile. Seatbelts should be cleaned with mild detergent and water. The buckles should be wiped off and checked for ease of operation. Solvents should not be used, nor should the belts be redyed. Either operation will damage the nylon. If a different color is needed, buy a different set of belts. If a belt is worn, frayed, or otherwise damaged, replace it. Seatbelts are simple to replace, if you stay with original equipment. Buy seatbelt assemblies for your particular car and reinstall in the old holes, checking first to make sure there is no thread damage at the anchor plates. Ford and Chrysler installations are illustrated in Figs. 7-6 and 7-7.

FRONT-SEAT ADJUSTERS

Front-seat adjusters can cause problems if the car is operated by more than one driver (Fig. 7-8). The adjusters shown here are for bucket seats. Most bench seats are simpler.

Reclining seats can be a challenge to repair since the mechanism is a complex collection of rods, levers, cables, wires, and other little doodads (Fig. 7-9).

Rear-seat removal can cause maddening problems if you are not sure what direction to push and which way to pull. Usually pushing the seat cushion down and back will release it. Occasionally brackets, screws, and straps will be used to help hold the seat cushion in place. Raise the edge of the rear carpeting or floor mats and check.

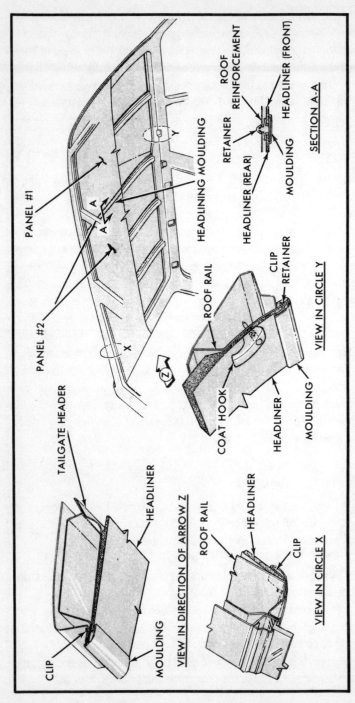

Fig. 7-5. Some Chrysler vehicles have molded hardboard rather than fabric headliners.

PANEL #1

PANEL #2

HEADLINING MOULDING

ROOF REINFORCEMENT

RETAINER

HEADLINER (REAR)

MOULDING

HEADLINER (FRONT)

SECTION A-A

TAILGATE HEADER

HEADLINER

ROOF RAIL

CLIP RETAINER

COAT HOOK

HEADLINER

MOULDING

VIEW IN CIRCLE Y

CLIP

MOULDING

HEADLINER

VIEW IN DIRECTION OF ARROW Z

ROOF RAIL

HEADLINER

CLIP

VIEW IN CIRCLE X

SEAT COVERS

Begin seat-cover installation by removing the seats. If the seat is a folding bucket or a split-back bench, it should be disassembled, as shown in Fig. 7-10.

The new seat cover is then stretched as tightly as possible over the seat bottom, and hog rings—heavy wire clips—are used to

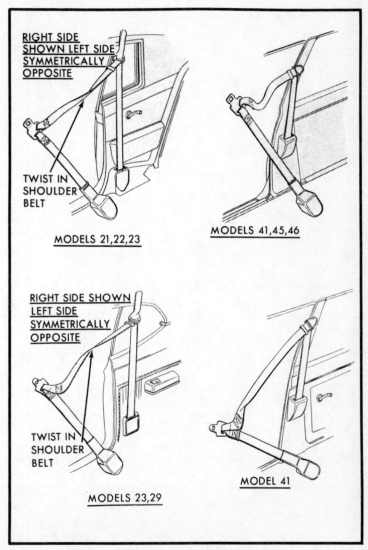

Fig. 7-6. Typical Chrysler seatbelt orientation.

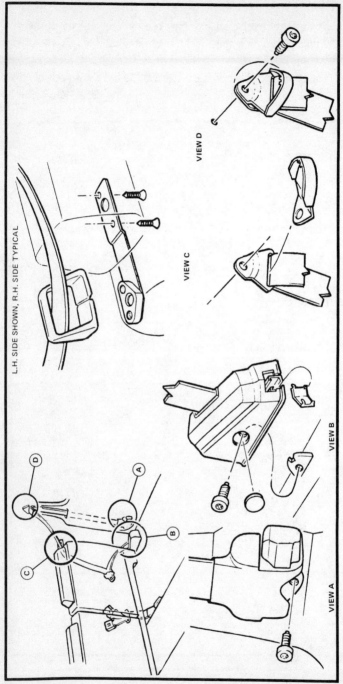

L.H. SIDE SHOWN, R.H. SIDE TYPICAL

VIEW A

VIEW B

VIEW C

VIEW D

Fig. 7-7. Two-door Ford seatbelt assemblies.

secure the fabric. Fig. 7-11 shows cushion-cover installation details for the bench used in Thunderbirds. Fig. 7-12 illustrates bucket and bench-seat cushions for some other Ford products. Figure 7-13 shows seat back-cover installation for several of the same vehicles.

Rear-seat cover installation presents few problems, but note that both the back and cushion must be removed, and that a large number of hog rings is required (Fig. 7-14).

Some luxury models come with fold-down armrests for the front seat. These are recovered, with hog rings and (depending upon the model) adhesive holding the fabric in place. On split-bench and bucket seats, the armrest mounts to brackets at the base of seat; bench-seat armrests mount to a plate that is integral with the seat.

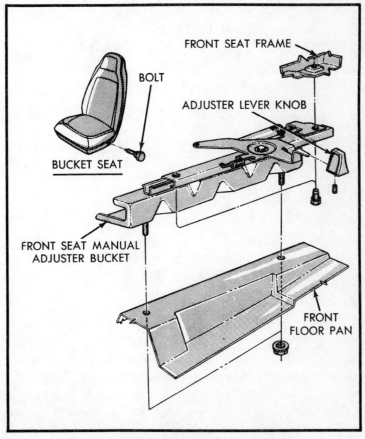

Fig. 7-8. Chrysler bucket-seat adjuster mechanism.

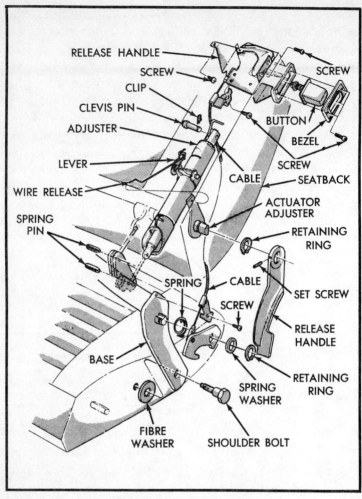

Fig. 7-9. Chrysler reclining-seat mechanism.

SEAT-BACK LATCHES

Federal requirements have mandated seat-back latches since the early 1970s. There is no truly typical installation, but there is a strong similarity among all. In theory the idea of an upstanding seat in a crash is good, and the concept has worked out well during crash testing. It is worthwhile to check the mechanism when recovering or replacing seats (Fig. 7-15). Assembly is a little tricky. First, the latch-return spring must be installed, then the latch and its lever are attached, usually with a retaining ring, to the front-seat back. An

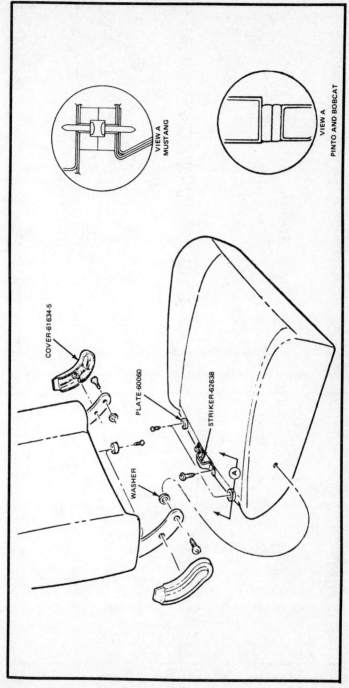

COVER-61634-5

PLATE-60060

STRIKER-62638

WASHER

VIEW A
MUSTANG

VIEW A
PINTO AND BOBCAT

Fig. 7-10. Maverick, Comet, Granada, and Monarch seat back and cushion.

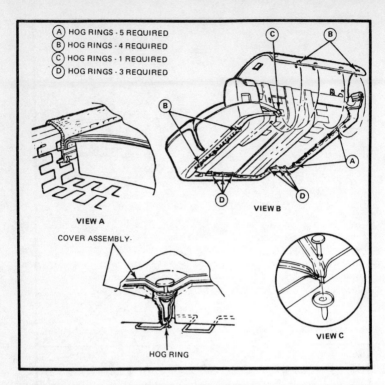

A HOG RINGS - 5 REQUIRED
B HOG RINGS - 4 REQUIRED
C HOG RINGS - 1 REQUIRED
D HOG RINGS - 3 REQUIRED

VIEW A

VIEW B

COVER ASSEMBLY

HOG RING

VIEW C

Fig. 7-11. Cushion-cover installation for Thunderbird and Continental Mark IV.

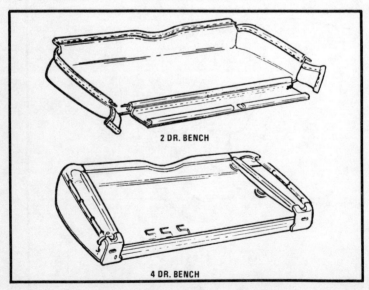

2 DR. BENCH

4 DR. BENCH

Fig. 7-12. Cushion-cover installation for Torino, Elite, Montego, and Cougar

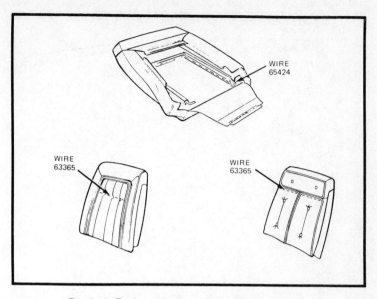

Fig. 7-13. Ford seat-back cover installation—typical.

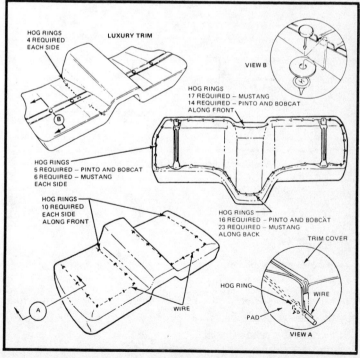

Fig. 7-14. Rear cushion-cover installation—Mustang, Bobcat, and Pinto.

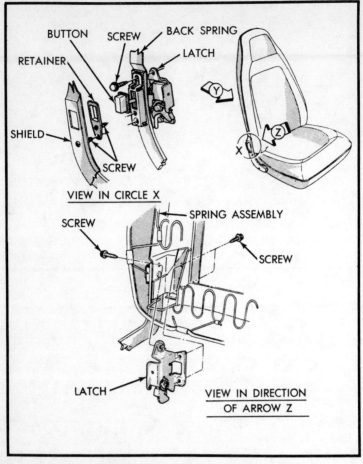

Fig. 7-15. Chrysler front seat-back latch assembly.

actuator is used in automatic installations that, because it is an electromechanical device, is a potential trouble source (Fig. 7-16).

CARPETING

For the average installation, the best recommendation I can make is to go to the auto dealer and order original-equipment carpeting. This standard rug material wears as well or better than anything else available. It is trimmed to size, and will have all or most of the cutouts already made.

The old carpet, if not too badly worn, can be used as a pattern for the new in the same manner as the headliner was used. Simply

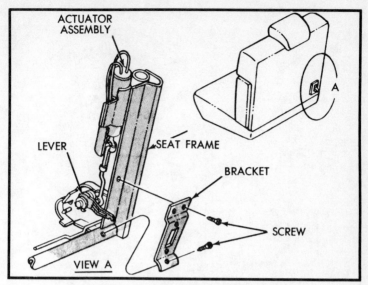

Fig. 7-16. Chrysler power-assisted seat-back latch.

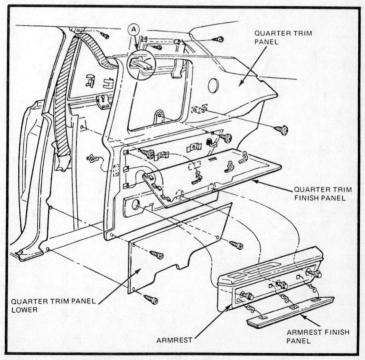

Fig. 7-17. Lincoln Continental trim-panel assembly.

101

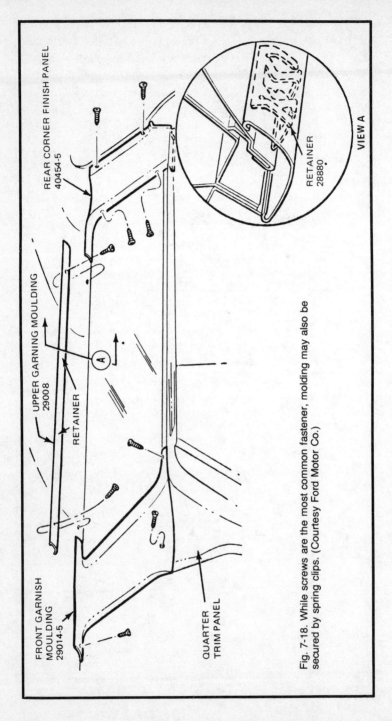

REAR CORNER FINISH PANEL
40454-5

RETAINER
28880

VIEW A

UPPER GARNING MOULDING
29008

RETAINER

A

FRONT GARNISH
MOULDING
29014-5

QUARTER
TRIM PANEL

Fig. 7-18. While screws are the most common fastener, molding may also be secured by spring clips. (Courtesy Ford Motor Co.)

remove the carpet (this will require removal of the seats, console, and scuffplates along the door sills—all rather straightforward jobs). Lay it on the new carpet and mark any holes to be cut with chalk. Make the cutouts and lay carpet on the floor. Smooth it carefully, install the scuffplates, reinstall the seats (and console, if any), and you are ready to go.

TRIM PANELS

Doors and interior quarter panels have trim panels secured by clips or screws. Replacement is simply a matter of getting a panel of the correct size, style and color, removing the armrests, and then unscrewing or unclipping the trim panel, as shown in Fig. 7-18.

MOLDING

Molding removal and installation is one of the simpler jobs. You need only be reminded that where a molding interlocks with another the second molding will have to be loosened before the first can be taken off (Fig. 7-18).

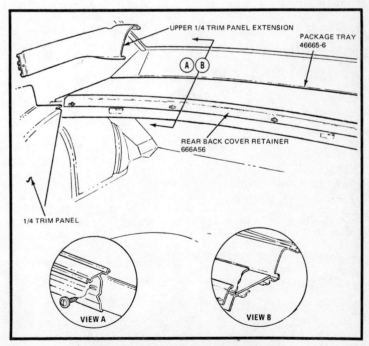

Fig. 7-19. Pinto and Bobcat package tray.

PACKAGE TRAYS

Though it is called a package tray, the sensible driver carries nothing heavier than a small feather pillow on it, since a hard stop can unload the tray into the passenger compartment. Still, with the sun shining through the rear window, package trays deteriorate quickly. Remove the rear-seat back and undo the mounting screws or, as the case may be, staples (Fig. 7-19). On some models it is necessary to remove the rear window molding. Installation is the reverse procedure.

Glass

A major part of automotive bodywork involves glass replacement, adjustment, and sealing. Collisions that involve the doors often damage window glass, and front-end collisions sometimes take out the windshield. Wear takes its toll of the window channels, forcing readjustment.

DOOR GLASS

Door-glass work is limited to adjustment and replacement.

Adjustment—Chrysler

It is essential that the door hinges be properly adjusted and that the weatherstrip be in reasonable condition and correctly installed.

First, run the window to its fully raised position. Open the door and remove the interior door paneling and trim, including the window cranks. Special tools are needed to release the cranks: GM cars require a clip releaser that fits between the crank base and the trim, while Chrysler products require a special screwdriver.

Close the vent-wing assembly, if the car has one. Tilt the assembly forward, rotating it around the spacer and, in late model Chrysler products, a T-bolt, until an adequate seal is obtained (Fig. 8-1). Tighten all nuts and screws. There is a torque specification for these fasteners. Check with your car dealer.

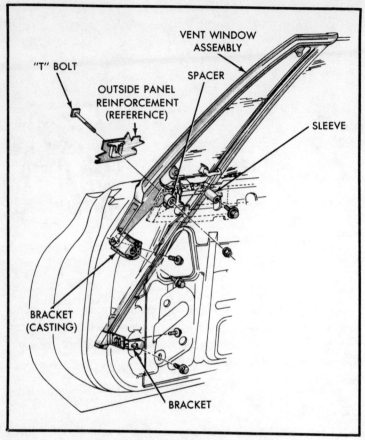

Fig. 8-1. Chrysler door-window mechanism.

The side glasses have a somewhat more complex mechanism (Fig. 8-2). Loosen the two screws that secure the run channel. One screw is visible with the door open; the other can be seen when the trim panel is removed. Crank the window full up. Tighten the upper screw that fixes the upper limit of glass extension.

Lower the glass full down and tilt the run channel back and forth at its lower bracket to engage the rear edge of the glass in its channel. Tighten the lower channel screw to maintain this adjustment.

Next, the glass stabilizer must be moved outboard to contact the glass. Tighten the stabilizer-retaining screws.

Cycle the window up and down and check for binds and slips. If trouble occurs, look for possible misalignment between the run channel and the lift bar. These parts should be as close to parallel as possible. Readjust until binding disappears.

Unvented Chrysler windows require a different adjustment procedure. The glass is raised until there is an inch gap between the top edge of the glass and the upper weather seal (Fig. 8-3). The pivot guide is adjusted until the top of the glass is parallel to the weather seal. Tighten the pivot-guide nuts. Adjust the rear track on its upper bracket so the forward edge of the glass contacts the pillar seal. Verify that the plastic liners on the trim bracket and its support contact the front and rear hooks on the lift channel, and that the glass stabilizers are in place between the glass and trim bracket and

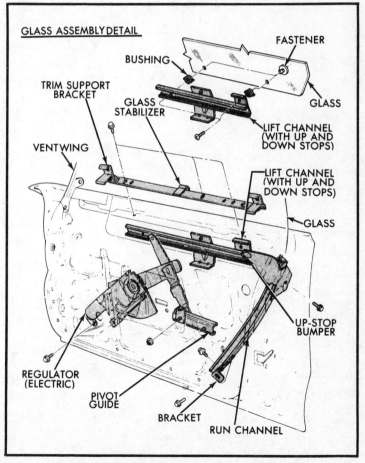

Fig. 8-2. Chrysler windows are bolted to the lift channel.

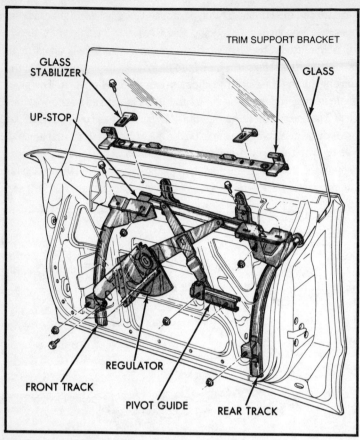

Fig. 8-3. Ventless windows have a more complex articulation than the vented types. (Courtesy Chrysler Corp.)

support. While maintaining hook/liner contact, position the glass and bracket outboard at the belt (or lower) weather seal and inside of the glass stabilizer. Position the inboard edge of the glass against the roof-rail weather seal. Tighten the front and rear track bracket-retaining screws and lower bracket-retaining nut. Check operation and readjust as necessary.

REPLACEMENT

To remove the glass, retract it to the full-down position. The trim-bracket support and glass stabilizers are removed. Then the screws holding the glass-lift channel to the glass are removed. The glass is pulled up and out through the belt, with care being taken not to damage the front and rear sliders, or tracks. The rest of the slide assembly is removed from the glass, and any lift-channel fasteners that are removed are discarded.

For installation, the rear-slide assembly, lift-channel fastener, and bushing are fastened to the new glass. The glass is slipped down into the belt opening. Again be careful of damage, and also make sure that the slide enters the flared top of the rear track. The trim-support bracket and glass stabilizers are now installed, and the window can be adjusted as already described.

To remove a door-glass regulator, drop the glass to the full-down position. Remove the screws attaching the glass-lift channel to the glass, as well as the screws attaching the regulator to the inside panel. Disengage the pivot arm from the pivot guide. If you do not want to readjust the glass upon reassembly, do not disturb the pivot-guide position at this time. If the window is electrically operated, disconnect the leads, and remove the regulator and lift channel from the door through the large access panel, with the regulator arms folded.

Do not dismount the electric motor or counterbalance spring unless the unit is locked in a vise.

Installation is the reverse of the procedure described above, though specified torque limits should be used when attaching the regulator to the inside panel, and again when attaching the glass-lift channel to the glass (this last torque reading is critical, since too much torque can crack the glass).

Pivoting quarter windows are rather simply removed and reinstalled. The latch-bracket cover is either pried off or unscrewed, depending on the make. The latch bracket retaining screws are then removed, and the weatherstrip peeled back (gently) to gain access to the window hinge screws. On Ford products a pin holds the latch to the retainer. Use a drift punch to remove the pin, and then remove the retainer nut and bushings from the glass.

To reinstall, mount the latch on the new glass. Then position the glass in the window opening and tighten the hinge screws. Secure the latch bracket cover.

TAILGATE GLASS—FORD

Tailgate glass is next in items of complexity. To adjust, loosen the upper bracket adjusting screws and raise the glass until a fit is

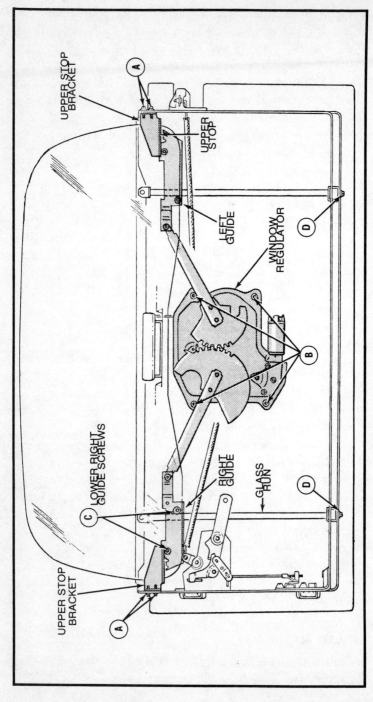

Fig. 8-4. Tailgate-window mechanism—Ford, Mercury, and Meteor.

obtained. If this doesn't bring the glass into alignment (the top edge of the glass should be parallel to the top of the glass opening, and there should be a good weather seal all around), the four regulator-attaching bolts must be loosened (Fig. 8-4). Now move the glass until its top edge is parallel to the window opening and retighten the regulator bolts. Once the glass has been positioned, move the upper stop brackets down firmly and tighten the screws.

For side-to-side alignment, loosen the lower right guide-to-glass screws (C in Fig. 8-4) and move the glass as needed to get a good fit. Tighten the screws.

To tilt the top edge in or out, loosen the lower run attaching screws (D in Fig. 8-4) and move the lower end runs backward or forward to get a seal against the top weatherstrip. Tighten the screws.

To remove the tailgate glass, remove the trim panel and the inner panel covers. Drop the tailgate to its down position and raise the glass part way. Remove the two screws securing each side of the glass to the glass bracket—see Fig. 8-5 for details of a tailgate-window mechanism—and remove all bushings and stops. Slide the glass out of the tailgate.

To install, position the glass in the tailgate and in the glass brackets. After making sure the spacers are in place, install the bushings, tops and glass-to-glass bracket screws. These screws must be tightened to specifications.

Adjust the glass and reinstall access-hole covers and interior trim.

STATIONARY GLASS

While stationary glass would appear unlikely to cause problems, the work can be difficult. The larger a windshield and the more complex its curves, the harder that windshield is to install without breakage. With windshields costing as much as $200, breakage is a serious matter. If you doubt you can do the job, the best bet is to take the car to a glass shop and have them do the work.

Most windshields are cemented and sealed in butyl. Installation entails careful detailing to assure that the seal is waterproof and that rust will not invade the metal under the windshield edges. You will need two large suction cups and an assistant.

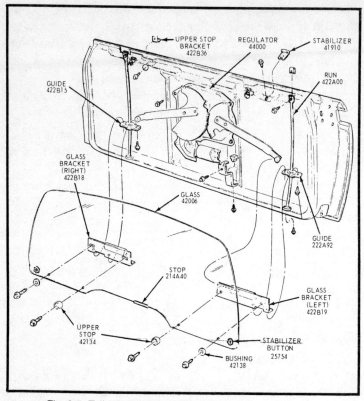

Fig. 8-5. Tailgate assembly—Ford, Mercury, and Meteor.

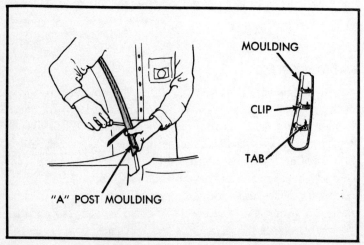

Fig. 8-6. Chrysler C bodies use windshield-retainer clips.

To make things more complex, some body types, such as Chrysler "C" bodies, have clips in the A (windshield) posts (Fig. 8-6).

In all cases, the area surrounding the glass, such as the hood, fenders and cowl, should be protected by blankets. Remove the wiper arms and exterior window moldings.

If the windshield is sealed with butyl, a 2-foot length of tempered steeel wire is needed—the wire should be no larger than 28 gauge (Fig. 8-7). One end of the wire should be anchored to a wooden handle (a piece of dowel 3 or 4 inches long is ideal). The other end is snaked through the butyl seal, and a second handle attached. With an assistant working inside the car, cut away the seal with a gentle sawing motion of the wire.

When the cutting is completed, place suction cups on the outboard side of the windshield and lift the glass out. If the windshield is to be reinstalled, it should be stored on a covered bench, well clear of the work area.

The butyl tape seal is removed down to bare metal, if possible. If bare metal is exposed, primer must be used before new butyl tape is applied (Fig. 8-8). Spacers and clips as specified by the manufacturer are installed (Fig. 8-10). Butyl tape can be applied either before or after the clips are installed, depending on the manufacturer's instructions. The tape is applied with its tapered edge facing the surface to be revealed and should lie smooth, without wrinkles, and butted square at the ends.

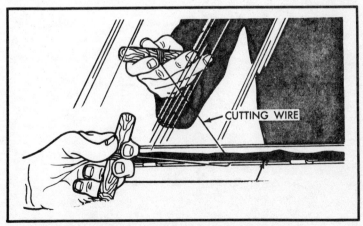

Fig. 8-7. Cutting butyl seals. (Courtesy Chrysler Corp.)

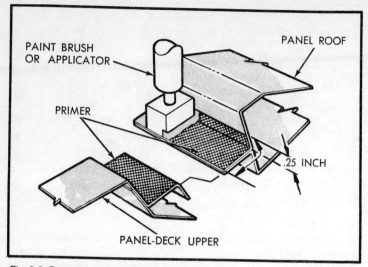

Fig. 8-8. Protect the windshield channel with primer. (Courtesy Chrysler Corp.)

Position the glass in readiness, and check for alignment. Do not lift it into the opening yet. Lay masking tape an inch or so back of the glass edges, so that the windshield is framed with tape. Once the glass is installed, the tape will help you square the windshield in the butyl seal. The glass-to-body-fence overlap should be equal across the top and sides to allow for twisting forces, expansion, and contraction.

The side of the glass to fit against the butyl tape should be cleaned with a solvent to remove dirt and grease.

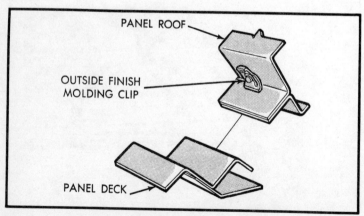

Fig. 8-9. Chrysler clips.

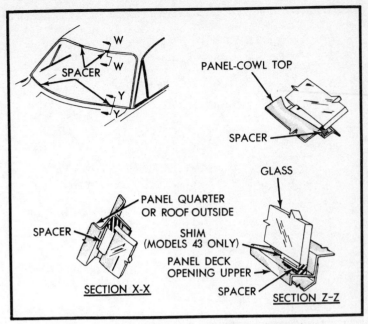

Fig. 8-10. Clip installation on one Chrysler body series.

Manipulate the glass into position with suction cups, making certain it rides on the rubber spacers. Figure 8-11 shows a typical windshield installation.

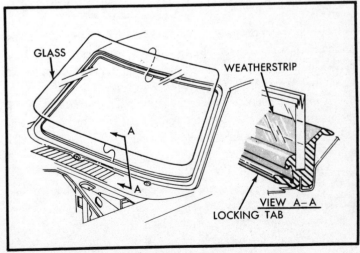

Fig. 8-11. Typical windshield installation—Chrysler.

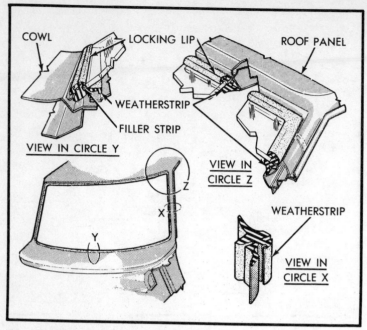

Fig. 8-12. Apply sealer to the fence and glass-groove parts of the weatherstrip. (Courtesy Chrysler Corp.)

Firmly press the edges of the glass into the butyl tape, compressing it to a height of about 0.18 inches. To check contact with the tape, look for dull spots anywhere on the seal surface. If such a spot shows up, press more firmly until it disappears.

Apply a bead of sealer around the outer perimeter of the glass and on the outer edges—those areas that will be masked by the trim surface around the entire windshield. Using a small wooden paddle, make sure the whole area is coated with sealer.

If you take the time to clean the interior surface of the glass, the sealer should set up enough for you to test the work with a light stream of water. Don't play a heavy stream of water on fresh sealer. If leaks appear, apply more sealer.

After installing the garnish, exterior moldings, and windshield-wiper arms, and removing the protective covers, another spray test can be made. If there are no leaks, the job is done. Otherwise, remove the trim and reseal.

Noncemented windshields are still used. Much of the job is similar to butyl-tape installation, with removal involving most of the same steps except that the weatherstrip can be reused. Weatherstrip should be loosened carefully around the entire windshield, and your assistant should support the glass from the outside as you apply pressure on the windshield. The traditional way is to brace yourself against the seatback and press the glass out with your feet. Be careful.

Once the windshield is out, scrape the old sealer from the weatherstrip if it is to be reused. In most cases it will pay to install new weatherstrip.

Apply sealer to the weatherstrip in the fence and the glass-groove portions (Fig. 8-12). A 3/8-inch bead of sealer is next applied across the cowl panel of the lower windshield frame. Position the lower section of the weatherstrip into the windshield opening, and, making a start at a corner, install the weatherstrip over the tabs, working towards the center. Press the weatherstrips securely against the fences.

With the help of your assistant, slide the upper edge of the windshield into the channel in the weatherstrip. Use a fiber tool to shoehorn the weatherstrip over the glass—do not use a metal tool. Using the palm of your hand, seat the glass with light, glancing blows.

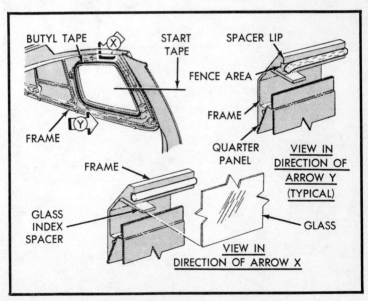

Fig. 8-13. Chrysler quarter-panel window using butyl tape.

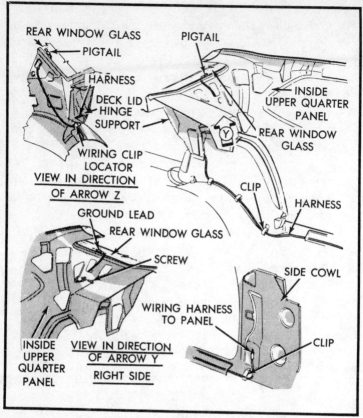

Fig. 8-14. Chrysler heated window installation.

Insert the fiber tool between the weatherstrip and glass at each corner, and slide the tool across the windshield.

Water test the installation and install exterior and garnish moldings and wiper arms.

Stationary glass for rear windows and quarter panels is installed in much the same manner. The windshield is the most difficult, so that has been my emphasis here. Figures 8-13 and 8-14 cover two other installations, including a heated rear window.

Body Fillers

9

Surface smoothness contributes to the appearance of the paint job. Several new materials have arrived in the past few years that make the job a lot simpler than it used to be, and enable the home craftsman to turn out professional-quality work. In fact, because of the care many skilled amateurs put into their work, there is a chance that the finished job will look better than the same work done at a body shop.

Of particular interest are the epoxy body fillers that are easier to use than the older, but still quite useful, body-filler leads or solders. One company, Arno Adhesive Aids, has introduced a tape that can save time and energy when filling holes.

No matter what is said, though, about body fillers, we must remember that overdependence on them will result in a poor job. There is no substitute for hammer and dolly work when dent-dinging time comes.

LEAD

While lead is harder to apply than other fillers, we should realize that lead has a purpose in the scheme of things. Lead is used in new cars to fill seams in the top and quarter panels, the cowl and front fenders, and in a number of other places. The amount of lead used is quite small and this should be a reminder to the home craftsman. Too much lead is worse than too little.

Body leads are alloyed so that they do not change immediately from solids to liquids as heat is applied. At 360 ° F most leads soften and become more plastic as the temperature is increased. The more tin the mixture contains, the more quickly it will become a liquid. Lead melts at 620 ° F, while tin in its pure state has a melting point of only 445 ° F. Most body shops prefer 70/30 lead-tin alloy. The melting point of 70-30 is approximately 500 ° F, giving a fairly wide temperature span between the workable and the liquid states.

The surface to be filled should be treated as if it were being prepared for painting. All rust, welding scale, and grease must be removed for proper adhesion.

Use an open-coat disc on your sander to take off paint around the work area, making sure to clean off an area larger than the area to be leaded. When large panels must be leaded, have an area 10 % or so larger than the work area. On smaller jobs, the cleaned area may be half again as large as the work area. The space is needed to blend the leaded portion in with the undamaged surface.

If the work area has nicks and depressions, a cup-shaped wire brush can be chucked into a drill motor and used to remove paint, rust, and weld scale.

The work area must be bright and clean before it is tinned. If this is not done, and carefully done, the tinning will not take and the lead will eventually crack.

After rust, dirt, and scale are removed, the metal must be degreased. This is best done with a degreaser used for paint preparation. Some of these products contain muriatic acid and etch the metal for better adhesion. Wash off with water.

Applying tinning flux is your next step. Do not use the flux sold for general-purpose soldering. Obtain body-leading flux which is a mix of the correct flux and powdered lead. As it is heated the lead drops out to make the tinning coat.

Tinning can be done with a rag or a wad of steel wool—but don't try to use the type of steel wool sold in supermarkets. It will break up and leave little chips in the tinned surface. Wear heavy leather-palmed work gloves to protect your hands from the heat.

Heat must be applied very carefully for it is easy to warp the larger body panels, particularly those that have a low crown. (Curved, or high-crown, panels are less likely to warp.) A propane torch is the safest choice: Heat would have to be applied for a long time to warp a panel.

Fluxing is done with just enough heat to make the flux react after it is brushed on. Tinning requires more heat, though still just barely enough to melt the small amount of lead used. Pass the torch over the work area in sweeping strokes, with speed acting as a control to limit the amount of heat.

Figure 9-1 illustrates the tinning process with a lead bar (and not with the lead-bearing flux discussed in the previous paragraph). The bar is held against the heat and the heat is applied until the bar begins to melt. A small puddle will melt off the bar, and then, as heat is removed, the bar will crumble a bit and you can twist if off the panel. This process should be repeated until a third of the area to be filled has small mounds of lead on its surface. Next, the area around one or two of these mounds is heated until the lead develops a sheen. Now wipe lead over the panel with a rag or steel wool. All strokes should be made in the same direction, overlapped to tin the entire surface. Continue heating and wiping until the surface takes on a dull appearance.

When the time comes to fill you will need more than small mounds to work with. The best method of keeping lead ready to apply to the sheet metal surface is to use a melting pot. The pot makes it much easier for you to keep the lead at the correct temperature, since you can play the torch over the pot whenever the torch doesn't need to be directed at the work surface. This tactic provides enough heat to keep the lead plastic without thinning it to the consistency of water.

For those of you who prefer to work directly with bar lead, you first have to control the heat. A propane torch will be okay if

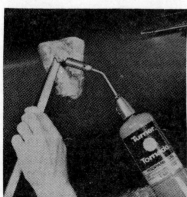

Fig. 9-1. Tinning with a Turner torch.

operated at maximum output, but an oxy-acetylene torch must be adjusted to burn cooler than usual in order to avoid panel warp. Turn the acetylene on and just crack the oxygen. The type of flame needed is long and fuzzy, with an irregular blue cone, tipped in yellow. This soft flame helps keep the heat down, but you should still make use of no more than the very end of the flame.

Using a paddle that feels good to your hand, and one shaped reasonably like the panel, will make the job easier. While the lead filler is being paddled, heat must be applied to the surface, but—at the risk of belaboring the point—heat must be applied correctly. The torch is held so that the tip of the flame touches the work surface, covering both sheet metal and lead, and the flame must be kept moving over an area that can be covered with three or four strokes of the hardwood paddle.

As soon as the lead begins to take on a bright and shiny appearance, it is ready to be worked, and heat should be kept to a minimum. For best results, the paddle should be used to pull the lead, with the leading edge of the paddle raised so that application is as smooth as possible at the start of the stroke. Pulling semi-hard lead over the surface will require more finishing work when the time comes to grind and sand.

Too much heat coarsens the grain of the lead. Work as rapidly as possible, consistent with good results. If minor panel distortion becomes apparent, wait for the lead to cool slightly—don't try this little trick when the lead is hot, or it will pop off the panel—and use a sponge to throw water on the leaded surface. The rapid temperature change should shrink the panel.

Your finished—that is, paddle-finished—surface should stand higher than the surrounding sheet metal so that filing will make the repair unnoticeable.

Since lead is softer and cuts more quickly than sheet metal, a grinder is not recommended for finish work. Instead, use a body file. Start filing at the edges of the filled area, and work in towards the middle of the lead for best results. Starting from the middle often results in too much filler being cut away in that area. Filing should blend the filler edges smoothly with the panel. Small nicks can be covered with body putty and sanded lightly.

Medium-grit, open-coat sandpaper is used to block sand the area. Use a grit heavy enough to remove file marks, but fine enough to be safe. You should be intent on getting the filled surface in shape for final refinishing, and should have already completed any shaping to contour that was needed with the body file. Don't use a disc or oscillating sander on lead unless you wear a respirator; a power sander will fill the air with lead dust, which is lethal.

EPOXY FILLERS

While some people think that plastic body fillers and fiberglass are the same thing, there are worlds of difference between the two products. Plastic fillers, including the increasingly popular epoxy compounds, are substitutes for lead body fillers, while fiberglass is used to repair large rusted-out areas, to repair Corvette, Saab, and other fiberglass bodies and to make replacement panels. For this reason, I have written a chapter on fiberglass, and will confine this chapter to fillers.

Selecting a filler can be complex since there are dozens of companies making these materials, some of which are available only in specific locales. To simplify your selection, go to a body shop and ask which brand they prefer. Generally you can trust the major brands, those distributed by chain stores and large automotive-paint dealers.

Less skill is needed with plastic body fillers than with lead filler, but the plastics cannot always do as good a job as lead. Some paints soften plastic filler, and primer/surfacers must be selected with this in mind. Lead is mechanically stronger than plastic and can tolerate some panel flex. Dust hazards are at least as great as they are with

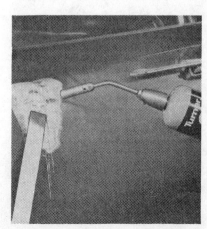

Fig. 9-2. The first stage of leading is to deposit lumps of the metal on the work surface. (Courtesy Turner Co., Div. of Olin Corp.)

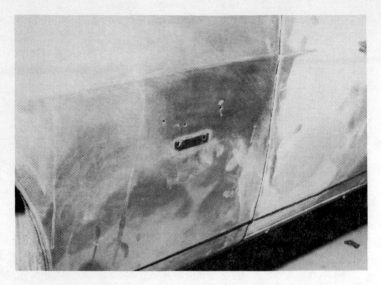

Fig. 9-3. Sand the paint off beyond the working surface.

lead fillers, so that a respirator should be worn when a power sander is used.

Most plastic fillers take at least half an hour to become hard enough to be worked, so the bodyworker has ample time to finish the area. Another advantage is that unlike lead, plastic fillers do not develop coarse grain patterns as they are worked. Thus you can change the surface contour several times using a squeegee without major problems.

The work area must be free of rust, dirt, grease and welding scale before filling. Use a hand-held wire brush to get off the heavy stuff and then use a cupped-wire brush chucked in a drill motor to get into nicks, cracks, and crevices. Roughen the surface with a No. 24 open-coat sanding disc to give tooth for the filler (Fig. 9-3). Of course, the sanded area should be larger than the area to be filled, and the paint should be featheredged. The final step is the use of a degreaser to make sure no oils or greases inhibit the adhesion between the plastic and metal.

Epoxy fillers come in two parts: A resin base and a catalyst. The unmixed components will remain useable for a long time; mixing the two starts the curing process immediately. The less catalyst you use, the longer the mixture will take to harden, so that you can extend the working time of your mix by leaving out a drop or so of catalyst. However, it is much wiser to mix small batches according to the manufacturer's directions, calculating the amount of filler you will be able to spread in 5 or 10 minutes. Cutting down on catalyst is harmless unless you buy a filler that is super-sensitive and refuses to curve.

Thorough mixing of the resin and catalyst is imperative. Use a piece of cardboard to mix the filler as illustrated in Fig. 9-4, making

Fig. 9-4. Mix the resin and catalyst thoroughly.

Fig. 9-5. Apply the filler to the panel with a squeegee.

sure that the cardboard and spatula are grease-free. Application of the filler is made with a wide-blade squeegee (rubber is best) or a putty knife. Squeegees are available at most auto supply stores and are preferred over putty knives. A squeegee follows the body contours beautifully, and leaves a much smoother finish than a putty knife. Should the material dry on the tool, a squeegee is easier to clean than a putty knife: Simply twist the flexible squeegee to pop off the filler.

The filler should be applied with a twist of the wrist, moving down and to one side as shown in Fig. 9-5. The idea is to force out air bubbles trapped in the mixture.

Plastic fillers must set up before being worked, but they cannot be allowed to cure hard. Using a cheese-grater body file, see if the plastic has the right consistency by drawing the file lightly across the filled area. If the filler peels through the grates in the file in long, thin strips, it's ready to be worked.

The cheese grater is used to contour the filled area until it is close to the desired shape (Fig. 9-6). A very light touch must be used or too much material will be cut away. When the proper contour is achieved, the plastic is allowed to cure and is then block sanded with a medium-fine sandpaper. Use a wood block initially and finish with No. 200 or finer paper mounted on a standard, rubber sanding block.

In areas where there are large, shallow dents, even the best of bonds may not be enough to keep the filler from dropping off: In such cases, drill a series of small holes through the panel and press the filler in so it mushrooms out behind the holes. This technique will allow you to fill large expanses that would otherwise have to be leaded, though it doesn't make the filler any better able to withstand flexing.

Body Tape

Arno's Body Patch Tape is an item I've recently tried. It is used in conjunction with plastic filler, as a backing over large holes. The work area is prepared as usual, from sanding to degreasing. The body tape is applied to the hole so that there is a 1-inch border adhering to solid sheet metal. The tape is sanded and featheredged. Apply body filler over the tape and smooth. Body Patch Tape can't rust, since it is a heavy-duty aluminum foil. Application is simple, and seems to work well. Durability? I can't tell you now, but the repair looks as solid as any I've seen. See Fig. 9-7 for a shot of the tape being applied.

Fig. 9-6. The filler is shaped with a cheese-grater file.

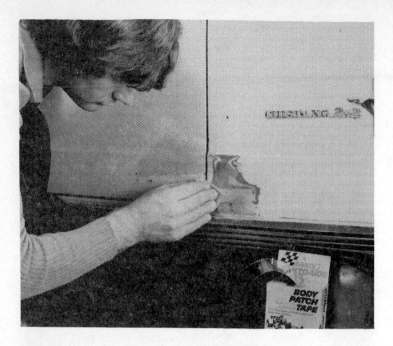

Fig. 9-7. Applying body tape.

Fig. 9-8. Ditzler makes a pour-type filler for shallow depressions.

Fig. 9-9. Used correctly, pour-type filler gives these results.

Pour-Type Filler

Figure 9-8 shows the application of pour-type body filler. The next photo shows the results that can be expected. While this job was done by professionals, it is not impossible for amateur craftsmen to duplicate.

Fiberglass

Most of us are familiar with the glass fiber used to insulate homes. After a do-it-yourself installation, we easily remember the fierce itching that went on for several days! This product is similar to the fiberglass used to build, repair, and customize automobile bodies, though there are enough differences to complicate matters. The glass fibers used in automobile bodywork are made by applying heat and pressure to small glass balls, or marbles. Long rovings, or fibers, are produced.

FIBERGLASS GRADES

Basically, three types of glass fiber are used in automobile work. First, and the strongest by far is fiberglass cloth, a cloth woven from the glass fiber or rovings, much as any other type of cloth is woven. The second product is fiberglass mat which, although not as strong as cloth, is used to supply bulk in the center of laminated parts. Third is chopped fiberglass, which is nothing more than glass fibers chopped small. Chopped glass is used as a filler for low-strength applications.

RESINS

Resins and their catalysts are essential. The resins bond the rovings to each other and to the automobile body. The chemical composition of the resin and the amount of catalyst present determine the curing time and have much to do with the strength of the material. Resin alone has little strength, but when fiberglass rovings are saturated with resin and bonded, the resulting section is exceptionally strong for its weight. Of the available resins, polyester is the type preferred for building, repairing, and customizing automobiles. Polyesters offer three distinct advantages over other resins. Application is easy, curing time can be varied at will, and the cost is relatively low.

Curing is the process that forms the hard surface on the fiberglass. Normally, the polyester and catalyst need to be heated to about 200 ° F for at least two hours in order for curing to be completed. Since most body shops do not invest in large ovens, another approach is needed to speed up the process and to keep costs down. One method is to add an accelerator to the resin to generate the heat chemically.

Room temperature, though, has an effect on curing time. All things equal, fiberglass cures faster on a hot day than on a cold day. In fact, fiberglass-kit instructions are not at all shy about saying that ambient temperature must be at least 65 ° F for the product to cure properly. For the standard polyester resin/catalyst/accelerator mixture used by most suppliers to the automobile industry, a 70 ° F day will bring the resin mixture to a set in about 45 minutes; 2 hours later the glass should be cured. Heat can be applied to speed up the process. Heat lamps (not ultra-violet sunlamps) should be placed no closer than 18 inches from the surface.

PURCHASING MATERIALS

The simplest way to purchase materials is to buy one of the kits available from auto-supply houses. These kits have matched catalyst/resin/accelerators, with enough fiberglass to cover several square feet. Kit coverage is indicated on the label. But most automotive repairs require two- or three-layer laminate strength. Keep this in mind when estimating the amount of resin and cloth you need. Bulk purchases of fiberglass cloth, mat, and resin will bring the cost down for major repairs. To simplify things, determine what you plan to do, how many layers are needed, and how large an area will be covered. It's better to add a layer and spend an extra dollar, than to make flimsy repairs. Take that information to an auto-parts house that specializes in fiberglass.

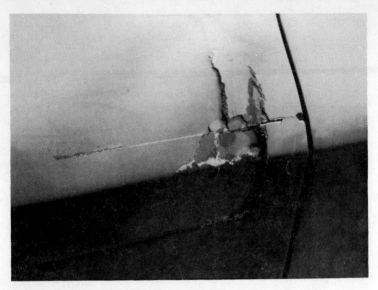

Fig. 10-1. Panel damage extends beyond the impact area.

Safety

Precautions are necessary when working with fiberglass. Both the resin and the fibers irritate the skin. You should wear gloves, especially if there is even the slightest chance you may have some sort of allergic sensitivity to the resin. For further protection, wear long-sleeve shirts with tightly buttoned cuffs and goggles. The fibers cause serious eye irritation and the resin burns like fire. Make certain all resin is cleaned from your hands at the end of each phase of the work. The resin should be used only in a well ventilated area and a respirator must be worn during grinding operations. Clothes should be washed separately, and the washing machine cycled at least twice to clear it of glass particles.

DAMAGE

A look at some of the characteristic types of fiberglass damage helps us to understand the repair techniques. Collision damage to fiberglass does not resemble collision damage to sheet metal. Metal crumples upon impact, while fiberglass flexes, absorbing the shock over a wide area of the panel, until the limits of stress are reached. Once this happens, the panel cracks or shatters. The cracked or shattered glass will always involve a larger area than the impact, as shown in Figs. 10-1 and 10-2.

Fig. 10-2. This Corvette was repaired by cutting away the aft fender section and grafting on another.

SMALL REPAIRS

No matter how extensive the repair, the first step is to remove the damaged glass, particularly at the edges of the fracture. If the cracks or holes are small enough to be filled without panel or replacement, the repair will be easy. Cut away the damaged material and bevel the edges of the hole. Grind off the old paint, going down through the gel (resin) coat to raw fiberglass.

If possible, this procedure should be carried out on both sides of the panel, for maximum strength (Fig. 10-3).

Lay out the materials in your repair kit. Cut at least two pieces of mat or cloth to extend several inches past the edges of the damaged area. Mix the resin and catalyst according to the manufac-

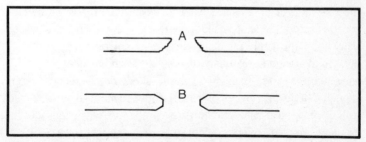

Fig. 10-3. The damaged area (view A) is ground out and beveled (view B).

turer's instructions, and spread the catalyzed resin over the mat or cloth. The glass must be saturated.

Coat both sides of the work area with catalyzed resin. One patch goes on each side. Press the two patches together and squeeze out any air bubbles. The resulting repair should have a slightly concave shape.

Allow the patches to curve—once the surface feels dry and hard, the material is hard all the way through. Curing is a chemical—not an air-drying—process. You may use heat lamps to speed curing time.

After curing, the surface is ground or filed smooth, and low spots are filled with epoxy filler. If additional layers are needed, sand each previous layer before the next is applied.

The process described here will work on fiberglass or sheet metal, though a small note is needed for metal bodies: Use polyester rather than resin. Polyester does not adhere well to steel.

LARGE REPAIRS

When the time comes to make repairs in larger cracks or holes, or to replace entire panels, you no longer have a choice between mat or cloth. The size of the area involved limits the choice to cloth (Fig. 10-4). Mat is only used as a strengthener and filler for the laminate.

No matter how large the area, catalyzed resin must be mixed in small batches. Not only does this prevent the resin from setting up before it can be used, it also reduces the fire hazard. Once larger repairs are under way, you will be working with enough resin to produce large amounts of heat as it cures. The liquid resin may ignite. Large amounts of resin, when mixed with catalyst, heat up more rapidly than small batches mixed in the same proportion. Try to mix only as much resin and catalyst as will be needed for each successive layer of laminate. Unused resin mixture should be disposed of before the shop is shut down for the day. A bucket of water should be kept handy for quick disposal of hot resin.

As mentioned previously, use epoxy resin on sheet metal and polyester on glass. Lay out a plastic sheet on the bench, large enough that several pieces of woven cloth and mat can be saturated with resin at the same time. After preparing both sides of the damaged area, cut a piece of cloth larger than the area to be covered. The amount of overlays depends upon the extent of damage: the

Fig. 10-4. The ground away gel indicates the amount of panel overlap.

larger the area involved, the more overlap will be needed. Saturate with resin. Cut two pieces of mat the same size as the woven cloth, saturate both thoroughly and lay them on top of the already saturated cloth. Apply resin to underside edges of the damaged area. Once the resin becomes tacky, apply the laminate to the underside of the area. Use the plastic sheet to work out air bubbles and to press the edges of the laminate against the panel.

To finish the job, a second laminate is made up in the same manner and applied to the outside of the damaged area. Once the repair is cured, file and grind to shape. Use flock or plastic filler to fill small depressions; sand and refinish.

Keep in mind that fiberglass is sensitive to paint. The paint you choose must be compatible. Otherwise the paint will peel and the repaired panel may soften.

STRESS CRACKING

Fiberglass is subject to fatigue—which is why this material is not used for chassis and suspension members. Unfortunately, some glass panels must bear loads and you may expect to find stress cracks at fender and door-hinge mounts. Repair the original damage in the normal manner and add at least one layer of saturated fiberglass cloth over the stress point. In most cases, this will solve the problem. When it doesn't, a wood reinforcement is necessary.

To add a reinforcement, grind the back of the panel down to bare fiberglass, directly behind the repair. Coat the section with resin, and place the precut reinforcement on the panel. Coat the reinforcement with resin. That should prevent further stress cracking. If it doesn't, the reinforcement should be backed up with several layers of laminate. That will cure it!

SHATTERED BODY PARTS

Pure resin comes in handy for repairing shattered fiberglass panels. The parts must be thoroughly cleaned and the original finish ground off without inflicting more damage to the panel. Clamp one of the large fragments into place. A C-clamp can be used on small pieces, but a cabinetmaker's pipe clamps are required for larger repairs. Build a "bridge" over the cracked area with resin. Continue the clamp in additional shards until the panel is jigsaw-puzzled back into shape. Work from the back of the fender, hood, or whatever panel you are rebuilding. Let the panel cure and give it a nudge to check for strength. If it wobbles, add more resin to the back. Once the panel seems reasonably strong, use an open-coat disc to smooth the high points and corners. The result is a thin shell in the shape of the original part. The next step is to get the strength up to par.

Using strips of mat, saturate them with resin and place them over the shell, working the material to remove the bubbles. If you want more strength, you can use woven cloth instead of mat. Overlap the strips at the edges. Finish as already indicated, starting with a medium-grit disc and moving on to a No. 220 or finer grit for hand sanding.

MOLDS

Sometimes the jigsaw/resin process is impractical because not enough fragments can be found or because the fragments are too small to use. If a replacement part is not available, a mold will have to be made. Here is where the convenience of fiberglass becomes evident, for the mold can be taken from another car or, if you prefer, a backing mold can be made on the damaged area, and a new part built up. In other words, the mold itself can be used as a part of the repair or you can use the mold to make a duplicate of the original part.

Male, or backing, molds can be made from any material that will take and hold a shape under a few pounds of weight. Hardware cloth or other medium-duty screening is entirely adequate. For unstressed areas, resin-soaked mat is just fine. For stressed areas, it is better to start with cloth, then add mat, and cap the job with another layer of cloth, all saturated with resin. Enough mat should be used to make the part as thick as the original. The hardware cloth will serve as reinforcement once the resin soaks in and binds it to the fiberglass.

For more complex curves, where a male mold may not be easily formed, a female mold can be made off the same part from a vehicle identical to yours. The panel from which the mold is taken must be coated with a release agent, or you will have major difficulty separating the mold.

You can use Butcher's paste wax or any other heavy floor wax for a release agent. Paste floor waxes will harm auto paint and you can lay on a much heavier coat than is possible with automotive waxes. Do not polish the wax out before making the mold. The wax should be damp as you lay up small pieces of mat.

It may be necessary to construct a two-piece mold. Curves that fold back upon themselves will lock a one-piece mold to the panel. And then you will have a problem.

Saturate the mat thoroughly with resin, and lay it on the waxed surface, using smaller pieces near the edges, and overlapping as if you were nailing shingles. Smaller pieces should be used on tight curves. The material should be forced into all crevices with a resin-soaked brush. Force the mat into place with the bristle-end of the brush; do not attempt to brush it in.

The mold is then fiberglassed on the back of the area being repaired. Use woven cloth, front and back, to hold it in place. Once it is secured, build up the surface to the original contours, using mat on cloth.

Another approach is to take a paper mache impression off the panel and use this as the mold for the replacement. This method is preferred, since the new part will be dimensioned like the original.

FENDER FLARES

There are two ways to tackle fender flares. The simplest is to buy a set of ready-made flares shaped to fit your particular car. J. C. Whitney & Co. offers fender flares for a wide range of vehicles. Speed shops carry flares for 'Vettes and other performance cars.

Flares are attached with sheet-metal screws. Once the flare is aligned and the excess trimmed off, the flare is screwed to the fender. Some owners install fender welt—the cylindrical bead still available for antique-car and Volkswagen bodywork. Another approach is to mold the flares into the body.

Grind the paint off the fender back an inch or so above the flare. Mix a batch of resin and chopped fiber, following the manufacturer's directions for catalyst-to-resin ratio. Back out the mounting screws, one at a time, and pack the resin/chopped fiber mix into the seam between the flare and fender. There are fiberglass "welding" compounds available for this job; check with your auto-supply store. Run the flare down tight on the fender, and squeegee off any excess bonding compound as it oozes out. Allow the glass to cure.

If the sheet-metal screws are visible, they can be ground flush; otherwise leave them in place.

Bond the outside surface of the flare to the body with fiberglass cloth. Make several laminates, since fender flares need all the support you can give them.

After the laminates have cured, grind the seam to contour, using a very soft, flexible backing pad and an open-grit disc.

Commercial body filler is now squeegeed on to fill low spots. Before it hardens, shape the filler with a cheese-grater file.

Use medium-grit paper to sand the entire flare and seam. If low spots exist, use more body filler to bring them up; reshape and resand.

At this point, use progressively finer abrasives: Medium to medium-fine to fine. Start with dry sanding and move to wet sanding for the final passes with No. 360 or finer paper. Primer-surfacer and the paint follow.

The second method for making flares involves heavy cardboard templates. Cardboard is easily constructed if you make small cuts around the edges for smooth curves without buckles. Tape holds the template to form.

The template should be backed with paper mache for strength, and should be coated with floor wax. Saran Wrap will work in spots where the wax soaks into the cardboard. Alternately, a paper mache mold can be taken for a smoother flare, since the surface of the mold can be cleaned up before laying the fiberglass.

Homemade flares do not have locating tabs like some commercially produced models, but with care, they can be accurately and evenly placed. Mounting proceeds in exactly the same manner as described above.

Spray Guns
And Compressors

The equipment you use to paint an automobile will add to or subtract from the quality of the finished job. Compressor and spray gun quality is more important than it is usually given credit for being. With too small a compressor the spray gun will never get the pressure to lay an even coat of paint. An inexpensive spray gun will make paint control impossible. The reason the equipment is of such great importance is the thinness of the final coat of paint: Just a few thousandths of an inch stand between success and failure—beauty and the beast—enduring quality and rust. It will pay to use the best equipment you can afford and practice until you've got the technique down pat.

While the proper technique will provide the essentials of the job, high-quality equipment makes it easier for the beginning painter to gain at least a reasonable degree of skill.

SPRAY GUNS

The spray gun is a tool using air pressure to atomize paint and deposit it on a surface. Air from the compressor enters the gun, mixes with, and then ejects the paint through the air cap in a controlled pattern. Most automotive spray guns feed from an attached material cup (Fig. 11-1). Remote-feed spray guns are popular in high production work (because the container can hold several gallons) and give the painter slightly better control of the gun (Fig. 11-2).

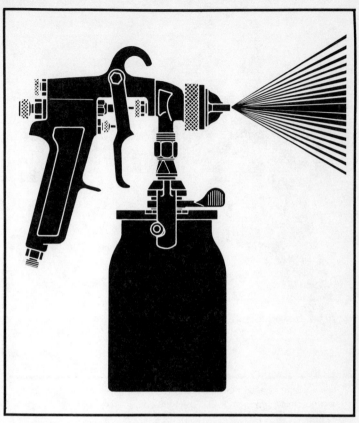

Fig. 11-1. A spray gun in action. (Courtesy Sherwin-Williams Co.)

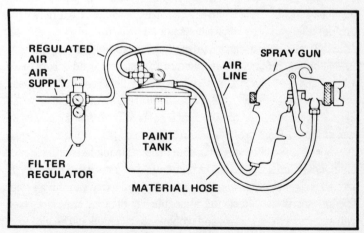

Fig. 11-2. A Montgomery Ward remote-feed spray gun.

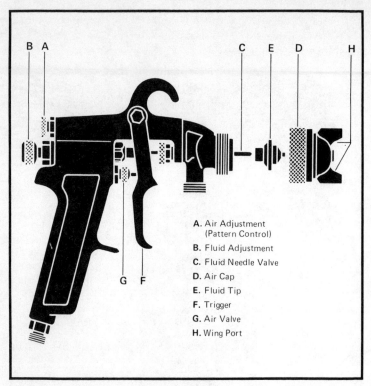

Fig. 11-3. Spray-gun nomenclature. (Courtesy Sherwin-Williams Co.)

A. Air Adjustment
   (Pattern Control)
B. Fluid Adjustment
C. Fluid Needle Valve
D. Air Cap
E. Fluid Tip
F. Trigger
G. Air Valve
H. Wing Port

Selection

Spray guns come in a wide array of styles, with prices ranging from as little as $15.00 to more than $115.00. Generally, the cheaper the gun, the less satisfactory it will prove to be in use, though some moderately priced guns will do as well for most of us as top-of-the-line models. Spending an additional hundred dollars or so will not add that much to our skill or to the final result. It's usually better to save the money that a really first-rate gun would cost. Of course this does not hold for rental tools where you should make every effort to get professional models.

Spray gun selection starts with the distinction between bleeder and nonbleeder types. Bleeder guns receive a constant flow of air, with the trigger controlling how much air is diverted to the air cap. The surplus is vented to the atmosphere. Bleeder guns are used with small air compressors and without storage tanks. The air bleed prevents pressure buildup in the gun and the air line. Non-

142

bleeder guns shut down the flow of air when the trigger is released. Nonbleeder guns are used when the compressor feeds into an air-storage tank with pressure-limit controls.

In addition, there are internal-and external-mix spray guns. The former is used with slow-drying paint, since it mixes air and paint inside the air cap. The external-mix gun is intended for fast-drying paint and lacquer, since it mixes the material in the air stream outside the nozzle. An external-mix gun will not clog as easily as an internal-mix type.

There are three types of spray gun feeds, two of which are of interest to auto refinishers—suction feed and pressure feed. Gravity feed is of little use to us. In a suction- or siphon-feed gun, the stream of compressed air creates a partial vacuum over the paint nozzle. Atmospheric pressure forces the paint up from the container and out the nozzle. In a pressure-feed gun, the paint is forced into the air cap by pressure built up in the container by the compressor.

Suction-feed, external-mix spray guns are used to paint automobiles, at least in the home workshops around the country. An external-mix gun will handle any type of paint from synthetic enamel to acrylic lacquer and right on to the two-part epoxies. Most suction-feed guns can be identified by wing ports extending beyond the fluid tip. A pressure-feed has a fluid tip that is flush with the sides of the air cap.

In addition to air-supply and paint-feed considerations, you should decide upon the style of the air cap. The air cap is the part that determines the shape of the spray pattern. While a fan-shaped pattern is most common in auto refinishing, other patterns are

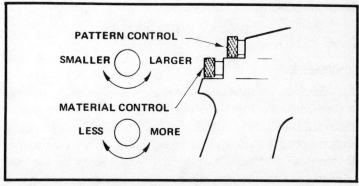

Fig. 11-4. Air and paint adjusters on a Montgomery Ward spray gun.

Fig. 11-5. A Montgomery Ward portable compressor.

handy. Determine the air caps available for your spray gun, and consider several, in addition to the standard fan pattern.

Adjustment

There are two knurled adjusters at the back of the gun. In the usual order of things, the upper adjuster controls the amount of air going to the cap and thus regulates the size of the spray pattern. The lower adjuster determines the position of the fluid needle which regulates the amount of paint passing through the fluid tip. Figure 11-5 shows typical adjusters.

COMPRESSORS

There are two basic kinds of compressors suitable for spray painting. A single-stage compressor has one or more cylinders connected in parallel to provide pressures up to about 100 pounds per square inch (psi). A two-stage compressor has two cylinders, of different bore diameters, and may have an intercooler between the cylinders. The cylinders are connected in series. Air is compressed first in the larger cylinder and from there moves to the intercooler for a temperature drop. From the intercooler the partially compressed air goes on to the smaller cylinder where it is brought to a pressure above 100 psi.

Your compressor should maintain a tank pressure of 80 to 100 psi. Fortunately, in home workshop applications, the compressor is used for one job at a time, so it can be smaller than the professional units which are intended to drive several guns simultaneously. The typical spray gun draws 8.5 cubic feet of air per minute. A 3-horsepower compressor will suffice. If necessary a smaller compressor, such as the Montgomery Ward 6425 shown in Fig. 11-5, may be used. However, the gun must be matched to the output of the compressor, which in this case is 6.4 cubic feet per minute at 40 psi.

Compressors smaller than this are inadequate for automotive work—unless the painter has the skill to make up for the limitations of his equipment. A unit such as the Miller 2000 cannot be thought of as the proper tool to paint an entire car. It has its uses, though, and costs much less than a full-size unit. As an air source for an airbrush for fine striping and other fancy work, the Miller compressor is excellent (it even comes with an airbrush). Such operations require extensive masking when attempted with a regular spray gun, which then will waste a great deal of paint and produce a poor job because of the difficulty of contol. The airbrush is easy to use and provides the control needed for the decorations and murals some owners consider essential to a paint job. The spray guns offered with these outfits are suitable for refinishing small panels, but do not give the control for larger jobs.

A friend, who works as shop foreman for Tom Gewant Ford in Kerhonkson, New York, tested the Miller 2000. He found the airbrush suitable for almost all airbrush work (Fig. 11-7), but felt that the spray gun would be difficult to use on anything other than spot refinishing. Still, Tom thought the kit would prove useful for many people. For more information, contact K.J. Miller Corp., 2401 Gardner Road, Broadview, Illinois 60153.

SPRAY GUN CARE

As I've said before, cleanliness is of utmost importance to automotive refinishing. You will find that spray-gun cleanliness is even more critical than in other areas.

Fig. 11-6. A Miller 2000 paint-spraying kit.

Cleaning

Immediately after use, the spray gun must be thoroughly cleaned. You should not wait even half an hour, for once the paint dries in the gun, cleaning is exceptionally difficult and occasionally, impossible. You may have to replace the fluid tip, needle, and air cap, among other parts.

Suction-feed guns are cleaned with the materials cup loosened and with the air-cap ring backed out two or three turns. Hold a folded cloth over the air cap and pull the trigger. This reverses the air into the fluid passages and forces partially dried paint back into the cup.

The next step is to dump the cup and rinse it thoroughly with solvent or reducer. Pour clean solvent into the materials cup. When the trigger is pulled, the solvent will flush out the partially cleaned passages. Use a solvent-soaked rag or a small fiber brush to scrub down the exterior of the gun. Do not dunk the entire gun in solvent, for this will remove needed lubricants and can cause deterioration of the gasket material.

Next, unthread the air cap, dip it in solvent, and blow dry with compressed air. A soaking in solvent will generally clean out the clogged air-cap passages. If not, a broom straw should be used to free the clogged passages. Wire or an oxy-acetylene torch-tip cleaner will change the size and shape of the ports, ruining the air cap.

Clean pressure-feed guns in accordance with the manufacturer's instructions. Experimenting with cleaning techniques can explode the cannister.

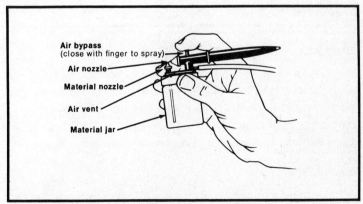

Fig. 11-7. The Miller airbrush.

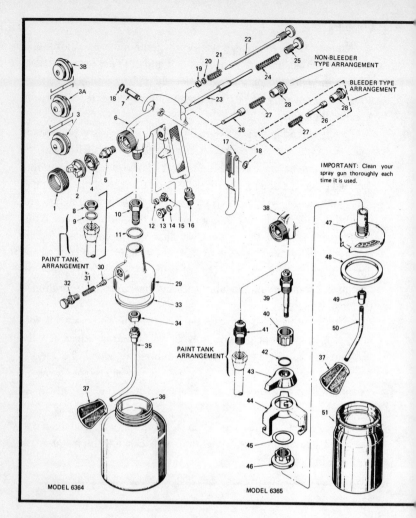

NON-BLEEDER TYPE ARRANGEMENT

BLEEDER TYPE ARRANGEMENT

IMPORTANT: Clean your spray gun thoroughly each time it is used.

PAINT TANK ARRANGEMENT

PAINT TANK ARRANGEMENT

MODEL 6364

MODEL 6365

Lubrication

Lubrication is necessary at four points on the gun body: the trigger-point screw; the fluid-needle packing in front of the trigger; the air-valve packing aft of the trigger; and the fluid needle at the lower adjustment knob. Use light grease such as Lubri-Plate 5555. The exploded drawing, Fig. 11-8, shows spray gun internals.

COMPRESSOR CARE

Compressor care is as necessary as spray gun care for two reasons: lubrication and proper adjustment extend the life of the

148

MODEL 6364 PARTS ONLY

KEY NO.	DESCRIPTION
6	Gun Body Assembly
8	Jam Nut
9	Jam Nut Gasket
10	Canistor Top Adapter Assembly Consists of the following parts: DH-530 Canister Top Adapter DH-563 "O" Ring
11	Canister Top Gasket
29	Canister Top Assembly
30	Valve Disc
31	Pressure—Siphon Spring
32	Valve Assembly
33	Canister Gasket
34	Retainer Nut
35	Material Tube Assembly
36	Canister

MODEL 6365 PARTS ONLY

KEY NO.	DESCRIPTION
38	Gun Body Assembly
39	Adapter Stud Assembly
40	Control Ring
41	Material Hose Connector
42	"O" Ring
43	Lever
44	Canister Clamp
45	Friction Washer
46	Clamp Riser
47	Canister Top
48	Canister Gasket
49	Retainer Nut
50	Material Tube
51	Canister

MODELS 6364 and 6365 COMMON PARTS

KEY NO.	DESCRIPTION
1	Lock Ring
2	Air Cap (External Mix)
3	Air Cap (Internal Mix)
3A	Air Cap (Int. Mix Round Pattern Optional)
3B	Air Cap (Int. Mix 45° Angle—Optional)
4	Air Cap Seal
5	Fluid Tip
7	Trigger Pin
12	Packing
13	Packing Nut
14	Packing
15	Packing Nut
16	Hose Connection
17	Trigger
18	Retaining Ring (2 used)
19	Pattern Control Packing
20	Packing Washer
21	Pattern Control Spring
22	Pattern Control Needle Assembly
23	Fluid Needle Assembly
24	Fluid Needle Spring
25	Fluid Adjustment Knob
26	Valve Stem Assembly
27	Control Valve Spring
28	Control Valve Cap
37	Strainer

PARTS NOT SHOWN

Allen Wrench 1/16"

Gasket Repair Kit

Fig. 11-8. Montgomery Ward 6364 and 6365 spray guns have many parts.

compressor, and if compressor is not properly maintained, the air coming into the spray gun may be contaminated by oil, water, or dirt. Contaminated air will cause major difficulties with the paint.

Basic compressor care involves little more than making certain that clean oil is in the compressor crankcase. Do not overfill—excess oil will find its way into the discharge air, particularly if there is no filter in the system. The motor bearings should be oiled per manufacturer's instructions.

The cooling fins should be kept free of dust and paint overspray. The air cleaner needs to be serviced every 20 working hours.

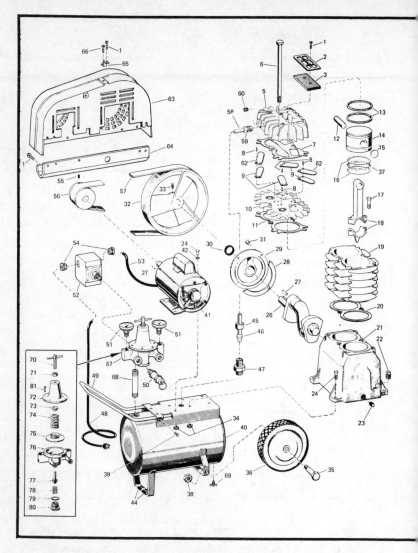

The air tank has a drain plug or valve on its underside. The tank should be drained each time the machine is used. See the exploded drawing, Fig. 11-9, for compressor construction.

AIR TRANSFORMERS

Air transformers are rare on small compressors even though transformers are used previously for spray painting. An air transformer keeps the air pressure regulated within narrower limits than

KEY NO.	DESCRIPTION	KEY NO.	DESCRIPTION
1	Self-Tapping Screw 10-24 x 5/16" lg.	44	Extruded Foot (2 used)
2	(12 used)	45	Compression Nut
3	Filter Retainer	46	Compression Sleeve
4	Intake Air Filter	47	Check Valve
5	Cylinder Head	48	Motor Cord
6	Hex Head Cap Screw 5/16"-18 x	49	Handle
	5-1/2" lg. (6 used)	50	Safety Valve Assembly
7	Cylinder Head Gasket	51	Pressure Gauge
8	Stick Screw 40-40 x 3/16" lg.	52	Pressure Switch
	Hex Head (8 used)	53	Pressure Switch Cord
9	Flapper Valve (4 used)	54	Strain Relief (2 used)
10	Valve Plate	55	Socket Set Screw 1/4"-20 x 1/4" lg.
11	Valve Plate Gasket	56	Motor Pulley
12	Piston Pin (2 used)	57	Poly V "J" Belt
13	Compression Rings (4 used)	58	Tubing
14	Piston (2 used)	59	Compression Connector 1/2" x 3/8"
15	Welch Plugs (4 used)	60	Pipe Plug Allen Head 1/8" 27 NPT
16	Oil Ring (4 used)	62	Restrictors (2 used)
17	Hex Head Cap Screw 1/4"-20 x	63	Belt Guard Front
	1-1/4" lg. (4 used)	64	Belt Guard Channel
18	Connecting Rod (2 used)	65	Belt Guard Bracket
19	Cylinder	66	Plascrew
20	Cylinder Gasket	67	Regulator Manifold Assembly
21	Crankcase Assembly (with bearings)	68	Nipple
22	Oil Filler Plug 1/4"-18	69	Drain Cock 1/4"-18
23	Oil Drain Plug 1/8"-27	70	Pressure Adjusting Screw
24	Machine Bolt 5/16"-18 x 3/4" lg.	71	Jam Nut 3/8"-24
	(8 used)	72	Regulator Top
26	Crankshaft	73	Spring Plate
27	Key 3/16" Sq. x lg. (2 used)	74	Diaphragm Spring
28	Bearing Cap Gasket	75	Diaphragm Assembly
29	Bearing Cap Assembly (with bearings)	76	Regulator Bottom
30	Oil Seal	77	Valve
31	Hex Head Cap Screw 1/4"-20 x	78	Valve Spring
	1/2" lg. (4 used)	79	"O" Ring 7/8" x 1-1/8 x 1/8
32	Flywheel	80	Regulator Cap
33	Set Screw 3/8"-16 x 3/4" lg. Sq. Head	81	Screw 10-24 x 5/8" (6 used)
34	5/16"-18 Hex Nuts (8 used)		
35	Axle Bolt (2 used)		
36	Wheels (2 used)		
37	Expander (2 used)		
38	Hex Nut (2 used)		
39	Sq. Head Set Screw 1/4"-20 x 1/2" lg.		
40	Air Receiver		
41	Electric Motor		
42	Washers 7/8" x 3/8" (4 used)		

Fig. 11-9. A two-cylinder Montgomery Ward compressor.

the tank regulator. The spray gun receives nearly constant pressure and paint flow is easily controllable. In addition, the transformer has a filter and water trap to keep the discharge air clean. The transformer is gauged to let the operator monitor compressor output much more precisely than he could with the tank gauge.

The transformer should be installed no closer than 25 feet from the compressor. Total line run should not exceed 50 feet. As distance increases between the compressor and the gun, resistance to the air flow in the hoses and pipes will reduce air pressure. If the drop is too great, the paint job will suffer. For instance, a 5/16-inch hose will cause a drop of 2 3/4 psi every 10 feet at a regulated 40 psi.

RESPIRATORS

Respirators are essential. All automotive paints are toxic. Two-part paint fumes are the worst of the lot. These epoxy paints will dry in your lungs.

Purchase a respirator designed to give dust *and* vapor protection. Standard types cover the nose and mouth and are generally considered adequate for occasional enamel and lacquer painting. Hooded types give better protection and are necessary when spraying epoxy. But no respirator is 100% efficient, and the spray booth must be well ventilated.

Now that your equipment is together—a spray gun that matches your compressor output, hoses, and a good respirator—you are nearly ready to start painting.

Surface Preparation

12

Surface preparation is the basis of all paint jobs. This chapter could easily be "How to Get the Most Out of a $39.95 Paint Job." Most low-cost paint shops use a reasonably good paint, sprayed with a minimum of competence (though seldom with more than a minimum). It's an axiom of the business that when a painter develops enough skill, he gets a job at a full-scale body shop. The problem is in the surface preparation. A fast wash, sometimes a fast sanding to break the gloss on the old paint, a quick and sloppy masking job, and the car is rolled into the spray booth for a coat of enamel laid on as fast as the spray guns will operate. That's about it. Surface preparation is such that most of these paint jobs may not last a year, and look pretty bad for nearly all that time. Compared with the five years or so of service we expected of factory finishes, this is a terrible showing.

A $39.95 paint job can be a good investment, if you do the surface preparation.

SANDING

Sanding can be done entirely by hand, although it's slow and tedious. The job requires No. 400 wet-or-dry paper and plenty of water on the final passes. It's much quicker to use No. 2200 paper and an oscillating sanding machine. Power sanding must be done dry! Electricity and water don't mix—even if the machine is double

Fig. 12-1. Surface cleaners, such as Ditzler Acryli-Clean, are essential.

insulated and grounded. Finish with hand sanding block, and No. 400 grit paper, and plenty of water.

Among the recommendations Sherwin-Williams makes for surface preparation is to make a very careful inspection of the old finish. The company recommends a cleaner to remove silicone (Fig. 12-1). Most automotive waxes contain silicone, which causes horrendous problems with the new finish. A magnifying glass should be used to check for minute cracks and scratches on the surface. If broken paint areas exist, the paint must be removed from at least that section.

Use a No. 24 grit open-coat disc to quickly remove the paint, following that with a No. 60 to remove grinding marks and to featheredge the paint that remains.

Stripping the finish off the entire car is never easy, but it may be necessary. If the paint has cracked or crazed, the only safe course is to go down to bare metal. By the same token, the new finish must be compatible with the original paint.

In theory, lacquer should be applied over lacquer, enamel over enamel, and two-part epoxies over virgin metal. In practice, you can fudge a bit with factory finishes. The original paint is pretty well inert because of the high temperatures generated in factory ovens. It is routine to paint over GM lacquer with acrylic or synthetic enamel. And you can usually shoot lacquer over Ford and Chrysler acrylic enamel.

Problems arise when the car has already been repainted. This paint is never as stable as the factory job, particularly if it has been air-dried. Unless the car is stripped, you are committed to using the same type of paint, although it is possible to spray "cold" paints over "hot" ones. That is, you can shoot synthetic enamel over anything, acrylic enamel over lacquer, and acrylic enamel and lacquer over epoxy.

Chemical paint removers are generally used to strip automotive finishes. The newer ones flush off with water, taking the paint down the drain. However, there are difficulties associated with these potent chemicals: Fumes are toxic, spills burn your hands, and any paint remover lurking in the body seams or window gaskets will nibble on the new finish. Its better to have the car sandblasted (even though you will lose plastic body filler in the process) by a specialist. A sandblaster whose experience is limited to heavy metal cannot be trusted around an automobile.

Bare metal should be acid etched so that the primer/surfacer will adhere. After treatment the entire surface of the car must be thoroughly scrubbed—residual acid will play havoc with the new paint. At this point, you are ready to tape, mask, and prime.

MASKING

How much of the masking is needed depends in part on what you have decided to remove. Semipermanent fixtures, such as the windows, and for most cars, the grille, must be masked. You should remove the bumpers, side moldings, nameplates, and other ornamentation. Door handles may be taped, but windshield-wiper arms are easily removed, leaving only the drive stubs to be taped. Most wiper arms are held by friction. Use a screwdriver with a broad, flat blade to pry up on the end of the wiper arm (where it fits over the drive stub), while keeping a small block of wood under the screwdriver blade to protect the sheet metal. Move around the drive stub slowly, prying gently. Other wiper arms are latched to the drive stubs, with the release on the inner edge of the arm.

A point to remember is that rust starts under the body trim, particularly where mounting holes are drilled. It does pay to pull as much of the decoration as possible to repair what rust damage is there now and prevent it in the future.

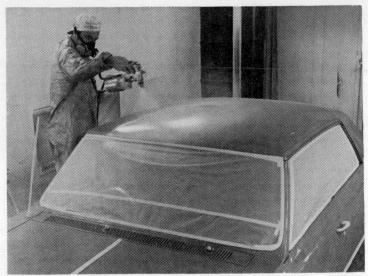

Fig. 12-2. Careful masking saves time in the long run. (Courtesy Ditzler Automotive Refinishes.)

Masking tape is available in various widths and grades. Beware of bargains—masking tape has a relatively brief shelf life. Many professionals use 3M tape because of its fine definition. Paint does not creep under the edges.

A single-edge razor blade or a sharp utility knife is used to trim the tape. The tape should be cut cleanly, without slicing into the old finish.

Windows are covered with paper. If you use newspaper, lay it on in several layers. Otherwise the bends and pinholes in the newsprint will bleed paint through to the glass. Make sure that the holes on the edges of the newspaper are covered. These gripper holes are present in almost all newspapers and can ruin an otherwise good masking job. Some authorities say not to use newspaper but with the above cautions you can save the cost of masking paper.

Completely edge the paper with tape all along the sides of the windows as shown in Fig. 12-2.

The same taping procedures apply to the windshield and the rear window, though even greater care is needed when wielding the knife or razor blade, since you will be cutting near rubber gaskets. Slice one of those very deeply and the car will leak.

Go over all of the tape before priming, pushing it down firmly for positive adhesion so paint will not seep under the edges.

Wheels should be covered by making a newspaper cap; leave flap hanging down to cover the tire and wheel (Fig. 12-3). Otherwise, overspray will color the tires and wheel covers.

If you are going to paint the underside of the hood, the inner fenders, and firewall, the engine should be masked. For the sake of thoroughness, it is possible to tape individual components (wire looms, steering gear, voltage regulator, master cylinder, and so on). The ultimate is to pull the engine, have the compartment steam cleaned, and make a complete surface preparation. This sort of work is done in concept with removal of the rugs, seats, door panels, and, in some cases, the dashboard. Fortunately, detailed stripping is confined to show cars, restoration projects, and super-sanitary street rods.

Once masking is completed, wipe off the surfaces one more time with a solvent to remove fingerprints. The amount of oil on one's fingertips may not seem like much, but it is enough to ruin a paint job.

PRIMERS AND PRIMING

Primers are first-coat coverings designed to provide adhesion between steel and the color coat. A primer is low in pigment content

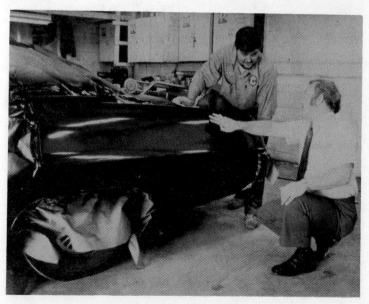

Fig. 12-3. Wheel caps should be taped in place.

and, consequently, is a poor filler. Surface imperfections will show through.

Primer/surfacers are used more often than straight primers. More pigment and some differences in compounding allow the

Fig. 12-4. Joe Bailey sprays a replacement fender with primer-surfacer.

bodyworker to combine priming and surfacing in a single operation (Fig. 12-4).

Because of its heavy charge of pigments, primer/surfacer must be stirred thoroughly. Apply in light, medium-wet coats. Heavy coats may surface-dry, while the underside remains damp. Eventually the finish pinholes and flakes.

Sealers are used to provide an intercoat adhesion, to hide sanding scratches and to prevent the original finish from bleeding into the color coats.

Apply in a single, medium-wet coat and do not sand.

Special primers are used where special metals are involved. Zinc chromate is needed to prime aluminum, and can be used as a base for several kinds of enamels.

Once the primer or primer/surfacer is on the car, wait for flash off, or solvent evaporation. Hand sand the entire primed surface with a fine (about No. 400) sandpaper, dry. Make sure to follow all body curves—use a flexible rubber sanding block on flat and low-crown panels.

Blow off the dust with compressed air, concentrating on the seams and moldings. The surface should be degreased again. (Many shops don't bother to do this, but degreasing takes only a few minutes and can make a big difference in paint durability.)

Primers can painted over a few hours after application. But better results are obtained by letting the primed car stand for several weeks before shooting color.

The finish will last longer since the undercoats have time to dry and shrink.

Paint Selection

In this chapter we will take a look at the characteristics of various types of paint and why certain paints should be selected over others.

Traditional automotive paints are divided into two categories—enamels and lacquers. Each of these categories is broken down into two more: Enamels are available as synthetics or acrylics; lacquers can be had in cellulose types and acrylics. Two-part catalyzed paints, such as Sherwin-Williams' Acrylyd-Polasol and Ditzler's Delstar/Delthane, are a category unto themselves, known generally as urethane or epoxy enamels.

Cellulose lacquer is the oldest paint in use, and urethane is the newest. We can ignore cellulose lacquer and concentrate on the other four types.

ACRYLIC LACQUER

Acrylic lacquer, used as part of a refinishing system, from primer/surfacer to final coat, offers ease of application, and quick drying time. Quick drying time is important to the home refinisher, since dust control is a major problem. The faster the finish dries, the less dust will settle on the surface. Among acrylic lacquer's disadvantages are the longer application time brought on by the need for several color coats, and the need to compound and buff the final coats to bring up the gloss. Cost is higher than for conventional enamels.

SYNTHETIC ENAMEL

Synthetic enamel is more difficult to apply and less forgiving than acrylic finishes. It is slowest to dry of all automotive paints, and, for practical purposes, cannot be compounded to remove surface blemishes (Fig. 13-2). On the other hand, synthetic costs less than other paints and covers better.

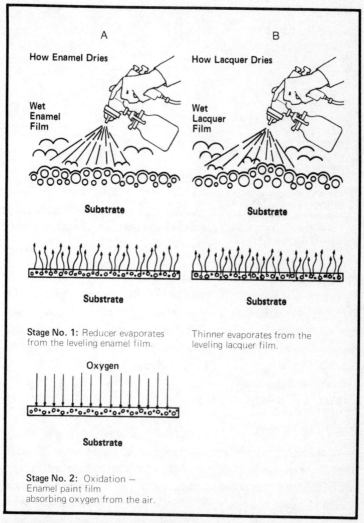

Fig. 13-1. Enamel dries in a two-stage process, evaporation and oxidation (view A). Lacquer dries when the thinner evaporates (view B). (Courtesy Sherwin-Williams Co.)

Property	KEM TRANSPORT Enamel System	ACRYLYD Acrylic Enamel System	ACRYLYD-POLASOL Urethane Enamel System
Color Retention	7	9	10
Gloss Retention	5	8	10
Drying Time (Tack free)	6	10	8
Taping Time	4 to 5 hours	2 hours	3 to 4 hours
Mar Resistance	7	7	10
Color Selection Range	10	10	10
Chip Resistance	5	7	10
Application Properties	10	8	9
Chemical Resistance	6	7	10
Cleanability	7	8	10
Wrinkle Resistance	7	10	10
Humidity Resistance	6	8	10
Corrosion Resistance	7	9	10
Appearance	8	8	10

Fig. 13-2. Comparison of synthetic, acrylic, and urethane enamels. (Courtesy Sherwin-Williams Co.)

ACRYLIC ENAMEL

Acrylic enamel dries faster than synthetic enamel and more slowly than lacquer. Nor is there need to compound to bring out the final lustre of the finish. Durability and color and gloss retention are excellent. Add to this quick access for two-toning—not more than six hours after the first color coat is sprayed—and the advantages become even greater. Cost is less than acrylic lacquer, but considerably more than synthetic enamel.

URETHANE ENAMELS

Urethane enamels cost more than other paints—currently $40 a gallon for primer and between $41 and $57 a gallon for color. The old finish should be stripped down to metal. Once the catalyst is mixed, the paint must be sprayed within a specific period of time. If the paint dries in the spray gun, you should look for another one, since cleaning is impossible. The overspray is lethal and you must protect your lungs with the best respirator money can buy.

Still, urethane is worth the cost and trouble for some applications. The chart in Fig. 13-2 summarizes the advantages of urethane. It is the best automotive paint going. If you plan to keep your car for more than five or six years—a good idea in this era of $5000 compact cars—or if you are building an exotic-fueled dragster, urethane is the best choice.

BRAND NAMES

Top brand names include Ditzler, DuPont, Martin-Senour, Nason, Mobil Chemical Company, and Sherwin-Williams. While these products are reliable, it is prudent to contact the body shops in your area and see what brands they use.

CUSTOM PAINTS

Custom paints are acrylic lacquers or enamels that have been mixed to give special effects.

Candy color paints are clear enamels or lacquers, given color with toners and sprayed over a metallic base coat. Preparation and priming follows normal procedures, and then a base coat of metallic is laid down. Candy colors are applied over the base coat, with each coat allowed to dry thoroughly before the next is sprayed.

Extreme care is needed to spray the candy colors. Standard colors, which are opaque, can be sanded out in the event of a run or other problem, but candy translucents cannot. The entire paint job must go, right back down to the primer! Touchup, for chips and such, is very difficult. But candy colors are beautiful.

Pearlescent and flip-flop pearl paints provide a really unusual finish, one that changes color as you move around the car. Pearlescent paints are difficult to apply, requiring constant agitation to keep the particles in suspension, and tolerating no mistakes. This paint is barely suitable for road-going machinery, since it is extremely difficult to touch up.

With both metallic and pearlescent finishes, a final coat of clear lacquer or enamel is applied over both metallic and pearlescent finishes. This requires sanding with plenty of water and No. 600 sandpaper, a wipe down with a wet cloth, and plenty of time for the water to dry. The finish then receives a mist, or kiss, coat of clear acrylic, heavily thinned.

Spraying Paint

The best, quickest, and simplest way to learn to use a spray gun is to befriend a painter. Unfortunately, not all of us can be that lucky, so we have to learn on our own by first reading this chapter (and any other material on the subject that is at hand) and then by intensive practice.

The more irregular the shape of the object you practice on, the better it will be for your skill development. Learning how to handle difficult surfaces at the start makes coping with large expanses of sheet metal child's play.

Collect some tin cans about the size of coffee tins for practice targets. If you can learn to lay an even coat of paint on these, you should not have a problem working around headlight openings, door edges, or any other part of an automobile.

I will also assume you have practiced with the scrap hood I advised you to purchase to learn welding and dinging skills. That old chunk of metal will continue to be handy. It can be stood upright to simulate a vertical panel, and laid flat for practice on horizontal panels.

At this point, careful surface preparation would be a waste of time. You don't care how durable the paint job is on coffee cans, though you are interested in getting a smooth finish. Begin by breaking the surface of the can's finish with No. 600 sandpaper. Degrease with one of the commercial products available for this purpose.

THINNERS AND REDUCERS

Thinning is essential for automotive paint, for as sold, these paints are much too thick to be sprayed. Thus we must first take a look at thinners and reducers.

The material used to lighten lacquer is called thinner. This applies both to cellulose and acrylic lacquer, though the thinner must be matched to the type. Synthetic or acrylic enamel is thinned with a reducer that must also be matched to the type of enamel used. Thinners and reducers are blends of active solvents and dilutants. The solvents thin the viscosity of the paint. Dilutants are neutral bodies that extend the solvents.

Thinners and reducers must be proportioned to the paint. The balance of the blend affects the flow during application and the drying time. Purchase paint and thinner or reducer from the same manufacturer. Don't attempt to save money with bargain-basement thinner/reducers. These products can cause trouble during application, and with the finished paint job. Too much dilutant (or "diluent" as some manufacturers term it) can make for poor adhesion, a brittle film coat, and chalking. If the wrong type of solvent is used, the flow

Fig. 14-1. Mix the paint well, filter, and add the suggested amount of thinner/reducer before the paint is poured into the spray-gun cap. Adjust the spray pattern. (Courtesy Miller Corp.)

and gloss of the top coats will be affected: Severe orange peel and blushing (see Chapter 15) may result from solvent incompatability; runs and sags will be present if too many slow-drying solvents are in the mix.

Ambient temperature is extremely important with automotive paints. Most synthetic enamels can be applied over a wide temperature range, but acrylic enamel is more sensitive and requires special additives at temperatures in excess of 85 ° F, and should not be sprayed below 60°. As a matter of fact, all paints work much better if applied at temperatures no lower than 70° F or higher than 80°.

The type of paint used for practice spraying is of little importance. At this time, just make sure the thinner/reducer matches the paint being used.

With the paint thinned according to the instructions of the label, it's time to strain the paint and fill the gun cup (Fig. 14-1).

SPRAY-GUN TECHNIQUES

Each paint has a correct spraying distance, or distance from the work surface to the spray-gun nozzle. Generally, the various enamels require 8-10 inches between the gun and the surface, and lacquers require that you move in until within 6-8 inches of the work surface. If the spray seems dry, move the gun in closer. If the paint runs and sags because the coat is too wet, move the gun an inch or so farther away from the surface.

Aim the gun at a clean piece of paper for one quick, full pull of the trigger. The pattern should look like the one shown in Fig. 14-2. Figures 14-3 through 14-5 show faulty spray patterns, and the

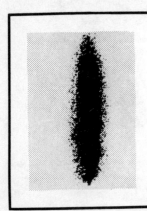

Fig. 14-2. The correct spray pattern. (Courtesy Sherwin-Williams Co.)

Fig. 14-3. A split spray pattern. This pattern is caused by excessive atomizing pressure or by over-thinned paint. Correct the pressure at the air-adjustment screw on the spray gun. Compensate for watery paint by opening the fluid-adjustment screw and slightly increasing atomizing pressure to narrow the pattern. (Courtesy Sherwin-Williams Co.)

captions indicate corrective actions. Minor problems brought on by improper paint thinning can be cured with adjustments at the gun, but major problems can force you to remix the paint. It is better to

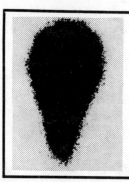

Fig. 14-4. A fan-shaped spray pattern. Open the air-adjustment screw to make the pattern-symmetrical. (Courtesy Sherwin-Williams Co.)

have the paint a shade too thin than it is to have it too thick, although there is no substitute for following the manufacturer's directions to the letter.

Fig. 14-5. A crescent-shaped spray pattern. Clean the air cap to open the wing ports. (Courtesy Sherwin-Williams Co.)

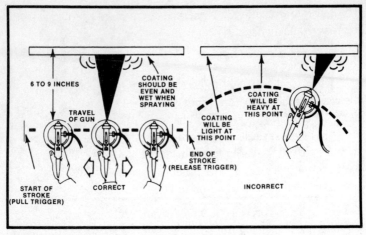

Fig. 14-6. Hold the spray gun the correct distance from the work and move it parallel to it. Arcing the gun will overload the center of the panel. (Courtesy Miller Corp.)

When painting a complete panel, move the gun parallel to the surface as shown in Fig. 14-6. The spray gun is never arced through its run when painting an entire panel, but it is arced if you wish to blend in a spot repair.

The trigger should be pressed before the gun reaches the work surface and released after the gun has swept past the surface. Besides ensuring an even coat, this technique prevents splatter as the gun is cycled on and off.

Each pass should overlap the preceding pass while keeping the nozzle centered on the lower edge of that preceding pass, as illustrated in Fig. 14-7. When the bottom of a panel is reached, the final pass is made with half the spray pattern striking below the work surface.

As mentioned earlier, the external-mix gun will prove best for your purposes. The fluid tip, located directly behind the air cap, meters the paint as it moves into the airstream. Its internal diameter is stamped on the tip with the larger numerical sizes showing that the tip allows more paint to pass. The sizes used in automotive work range from 0.070 inch down to 0.040 inch. Pressure-feed guns have smaller diameter tips than suction-feed guns. The fluid tip and its needle must match and the compressor must be able to handle the flow demanded by the fluid tip/needle combination. If your compressor is anemic, you should move down a size or two on the fluid tip.

The flow rate will suffer, but that is better than the alternative which is pressure fluctuation.

Blending

When painting an entire car, the overspray from one panel to the next and the slight differences of paint color as you refill the gun detract from the appearance of the completed work.

There are several ways to avoid this problem. One technique is to move around the car in such a manner that the paint on one panel hasn't time to dry before the panel next to it is painted.

Start at the roof, move on to hood, painting the entire hood, before going on to the right or left fender. As soon as the fender is completed, continue down the side of the automobile, stopping at the rear of the front door. Move to the opposite side of the car and paint the fender door, and rear fender. Move back to the rear of the front door where you first stopped and shoot the remainder of the car. If you follow this procedure for each coat of paint, or primer-surfacer, there will be little difficulty with the paint drying enough to show overspray or slight color mismatches.

Many professionals don't bother with the above technique for two reasons: Pros are faster than someone who shoots a car twice in a lifetime, so enamels do not have time to harden and so can absorb overspray; and professionals are experienced at covering up poorly blended paint.

Fig. 14-7. Center the nozzle on the bottom of each stroke. (Courtesy Miller Corp.)

For standard paint jobs you can expect to need three or four coats of acrylic enamel, and a half dozen coats of acrylic lacquer for a good coverage. Each coat must be as perfect as you can make it, for any imperfection will show up in the finish coat. If you are going to make mistakes, try to confine them to the primer-surfacer coats where they can be more easily sanded out and recoated.

Spot Blending

Spot blending is a skill that requires practice to develop. The need for blending spot repairs is obvious once the area is painted; the original finish will be divided from the new finish by a sharp line of demarcation, no matter how closely the paint formula matches the original. Most professionals prefer to refinish whole panels rather than go through the hassle of blending, but blending will save material and money for the home refinisher.

There's little difference between blending paint and featheredging lead or epoxy filler. What you are trying to do is break up the sharp outline around the repaired area. The odds are excellent that the color match will be less than perfect, but eliminating the sharp break tends to fool the eye into thinking the match is closer than it really is.

Begin with a single coat of primer which is allowed to set up thoroughly. Next comes a double primer coat, again allowed to dry hard. The final coat is a color coat, overlapping the original finish. Here we break the rules, and arc the gun at the end of the stroke to fade in color coat with the old paint.

Blending is assisted by a dust coat. The dust coat is a faster-than-normal pass of the gun that gives better control between coats.

Mist coats may also help, but should be used cautiously by a nonprofessional. Mist coats consist of a slow-drying thinner/reducer with a touch of color added. After practice, mist coating can become an aid in blending.

Blending is, of course, practical only if the original finish can be compounded and buffed to a decent gloss, with reasonable depth and little color fade. Otherwise, blending is a waste of time and energy. Your purposes would be better served by refinishing the entire car.

Troubleshooting And Spot Repair

Many things can go wrong with a new paint job. The troubleshooting repair procedures that follow are based on material supplied by Chrysler.

PAINT DEFECTS

Each paint defect has a specific remedy.

Bubbles

Small bubbles in the finish will normally be confined to a small area. Use Method 3 in the second section of this chapter for refinishing the affected section.

Chipping

Chipping is caused by impacts from stones or other hard objects, and can occur in any paint job. Method 3 will correct the damage.

Dirt in Paint

Dirt shows up as specks in the paint. Method 1—oil sanding, buffing, and polishing—can correct superficial damage. For more extensive repairs, use Method 3.

Dry Spray

Dry spray is caused by insufficient paint in the spray pattern or by overspray. Overspray is the more common of the two, and can be corrected by Method 1.

Dull or Faded Finish

Correct with Method 1.

Industrial Fallout

All kinds of goop floats out of factory chimneys, even in these pollution-conscious times. Washing will remove much of it, but Method 1 will sometimes be necessary. If the fallout is corrosive, Method 3 is the only alternative.

Metal Finishing Marks

Light whorls made by a grinder can often be removed by Method 1. If the marks are still visible, resort to Method 3.

Mottling

Mottling is an obvious condition—the density of the finish seems to vary. Repair with Method 4.

No Adhesion

Correct with Method 3, refinishing the area. Give careful attention to grease and dirt removal or peeling will continue.

Off-Color Paint

Correct with Method 4.

Orange Peel

Orange peel describes a condition where the surface of the paint takes on the rough texture of an orange skin. It is quite common, and in most cases can be corrected by Method 1.

Pit Marks in the Filler

Correct by Method 2 or, if a large area is involved, Method 3.

Runs or Sags

This condition can sometimes be corrected by Method 1. If not, Method 4 will be needed.

Surface Scratches

Light scratches can be removed by Method 1, but deeper scratches require Method 3.

Sealer Cracking

This condition appears at body seams. Correct by digging out the old sealer and applying new. Refinish with Method 2 or Method 3.

REPAIR PROCEDURES

Method 1 consists of three steps: sanding, buffing, and polishing. Figures 15-1 through 15-3 illustrate these procedures.

Spot repairs require Method 2. Mask the area to be painted and remove all traces of wax and grease. Sand (Fig. 15-4) and wipe the panel with reducer, being careful not to streak it. Blow off the dust, and wipe with a tack rag (Fig. 15-5). Shoot the color coat and burn in

Fig. 15-1. Wrap a piece of No. 600 wet-or-dry paper over a rubber squeegee and lubricate with mineral oil. (Courtesy Chrysler Corp.)

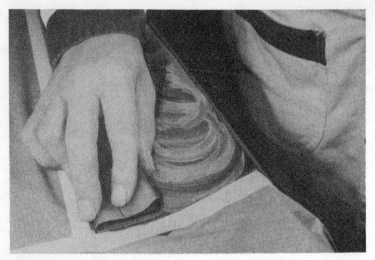

Fig. 15-2. Sand the blemish in a circular motion. (Courtesy Chrysler Corp.)

the edges of the new finish (Fig. 15-6). If acrylic lacquer was used, compound and polish (Fig. 15-7).

Sectioning a panel—rather than painting the entire surface—is Method 3. It is possible because panels on late model cars are angular with sharply defined breaklines. Wash the panel with detergent and rinse (Fig. 15-8). Sand the damaged area, blow off the dust, and degrease. Apply 3/4-inch masking tape so that it overlaps 3/16

Fig. 15-3. Compound out the sanding marks. (Courtesy Chrysler Corp.)

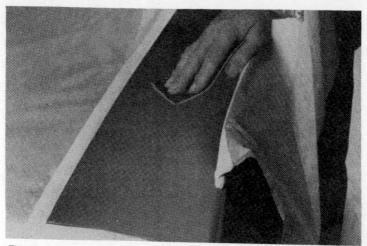

Fig. 15-4. After the panel has been masked and degreased; sand the old finish. (Courtesy Chrysler Corp.)

inch into the repair area (Fig. 15-9). Fluff the tape back to the breakline to prevent paint buildup at the edges of the repair (Fig. 15-10). Shoot the color coat (Fig. 15-11).

Method 4 is used to correct minor surface flaws. Scuff the repair area with No. 400 sandpaper, clean, degrease, and mask as described for Method 3. Shoot one or more color coats.

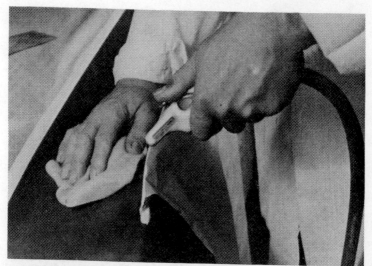

Fig. 15-5. Wipe the panel with reducer and, with a tack rag and air gun, clean dust and dirt from the panel. (Courtesy Chrysler Corp.)

Fig. 15-6. Apply the color coat from the outboard side of the panel inward. Blend, or burn in, the edges of the new paint with rich reducers. (Courtesy Chrysler Corp.)

WOOD-GRAINED OVERLAY REPLACEMENT

Wood-grained overlays are not impossible to replace, although the work requires a high level of skill. Remove the trim moldings and door hardware. Protect the paint on adjacent panels with masking tape and paper. Spray overlay remover (Chrysler recommends 3M brand sold in aerosol cans) on the upper panel. Spray a second time and allow 20 minutes for the overlay to soften.

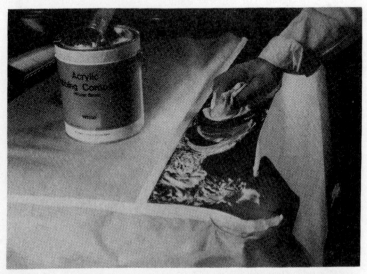

Fig. 15-7. If the repair is made with acrylic lacquer, compounding will be required. (Courtesy Chrysler Corp.)

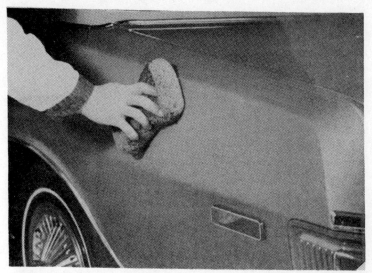

Fig. 15-8. Using a mild household detergent, wash the entire panel. (Courtesy Chrysler Corp.)

Peel the overlay at the flange, or upper, area at one corner (Fig. 15-12). If the overlay is stubborn, apply more remover, wait a few minutes, and squeegee the remaining spots (Fig. 15-13).

Once the overlay is removed, spray the panel one more time with adhesive remover and use a hard plastic squeegee to remove the adhesive residue (Fig. 15-14). Spray and scrape until the panel is

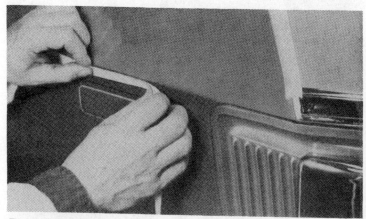

Fig. 15-9. Once the damaged area is sanded, dusted, and degreased, apply 3/4-inch masking tape to the breakline, allowing 3/16 inch of tape overlap into the repair area. (Courtesy Chrysler Corp.)

177

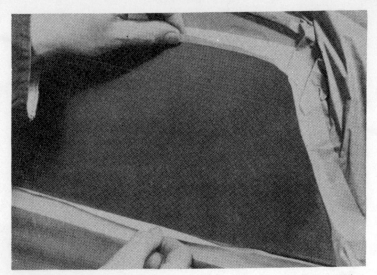

Fig. 15-10. Fluff the overlapped portion of the tape outward to form a pocket. (Courtesy Chrysler Corp.)

free of adhesive. Remove the masking tape, and wash the entire surface with 3M general-purpose adhesive and wax remover.

For best results, vinyl overlays should be installed when ambient temperature is between 70 ° and 90 ° F. Heat lamps can be used in cold weather.

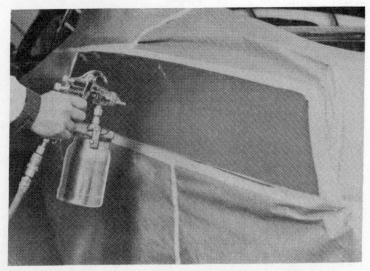

Fig. 15-11. Apply the color coat. (Courtesy Chrysler Corp.)

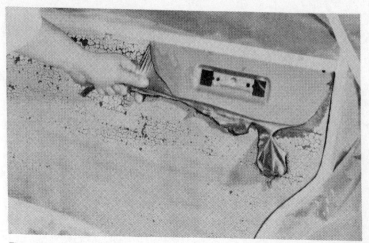

Fig. 15-12. Once the overlay is softened, pull it off the flange area. (Courtesy Chrysler Corp.)

The overlay should be cut 1/2 inch larger than the panel, and should be placed on a clean, flat surface with the backing paper. Hold the overlay firmly and skin the backing with a smooth, steady motion. Under hot, humid conditions, a slight jerking motion may be helpful. The backing must be removed from the overlay, not the overlay from the backing. The overlay will stretch and tear if pulled away from the paper. Do not touch the center of the overlay, because it will show fingerprints.

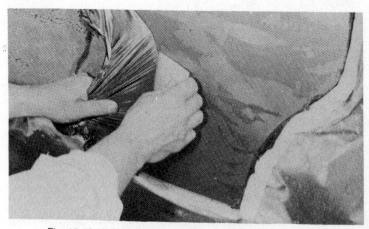

Fig. 15-13. A squeegee is helpful. (Courtesy Chrysler Corp.)

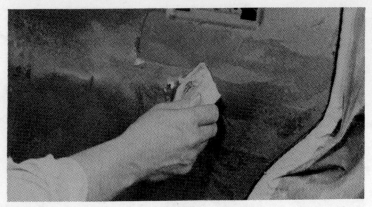

Fig. 15-14. After the overlay is peeled, apply adhesive remover, let stand for a few minutes, and squeegee the residue from the panel. (Courtesy Chrysler Corp.)

Add two or three teaspoonfuls of mild, powdered household detergent to a gallon of warm (80 °-90 °F) water. Wet panel and the adhesive side of the overlay.

Using a rubber squeegee, press the overlay to the body with firm strokes, making sure the strokes overlap to remove air bubbles, water, and wrinkles (Fig. 15-15). Start at the top edge first, then work down. Trim the overlay to the edge of the molding-retaining studs (Fig. 15-16). Allow a half-inch or so overlap at the panel edges (Fig. 15-17).

Squeegee the overlay a second time and dry the surface with a piece of clean cheesecloth.

To get good contact around door flanges, heat the overlay with a hot-air gun (Fig. 15-18). Note the way the edge of the overlay is slitted. Hair dryers work well here. Wrap the overlay around the flange and press it firmly in place (Fig. 15-19). Avoid trapping air when turning the edge of the overlay. Flatten the turned edge with a squeegee.

Inspect the job for water or air blisters. Small blisters can be punctured with a pin (Fig. 15-20).

Reinstall all molding trim and door hardware.

OVERLAY REPAIR

Very light scratches and nicks can be removed by sanding, since overlay has a clear plastic coating. But exercise great

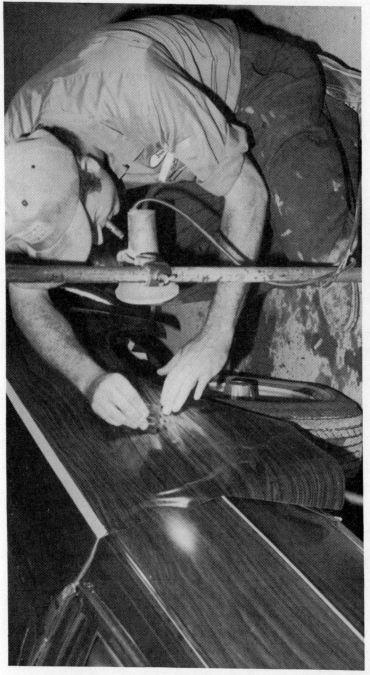

Fig. 15-15. Overlay is applied with a rubber squeegee.

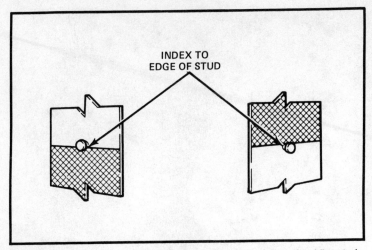

INDEX TO
EDGE OF STUD

Fig. 15-16. The overlay must be trimmed to index with the edge of molding studs. These studs secure the molding that frames the overlay. (Courtesy Chrysler Corp.)

caution—should you abrade the overlay, the entire section will have to be replaced. Use nothing coarser than No. 600 sandpaper.

Wipe the sanded surface and surrounding area with a rag dampened in solvent (Chrysler mentions naphtha but if this solvent is used, precautions are essential since naphtha fumes are both flammable and toxic). Using compressed air and a tack rag, remove all dirt and lint from the repair surfaces. Apply a topcoat of clean acrylic enamel with an airbrush.

Small tears can be repaired with good results. Use a small brush to apply a drop of touchup acrylic enamel to the damaged area. Repeat at intervals until the repair blends with the overlay. Allow to dry for 45 minutes, and coat with clear acrylic enamel.

BODY STRIPES

Most factory-installed stripes are glued on. Soften the adhesive with a heat gun (or hair dryer) and peel the stripe off. Degrease and dewax the panel.

Peel about 8 inches of backing from the replacement stripe. Align with the marks left by the old stripe.

Press the stripe to the panel, removing backing as you work your way along the side of the car. Finger pressure will be enough for narrow stripes. Wide racing stripes must be squeegeed on.

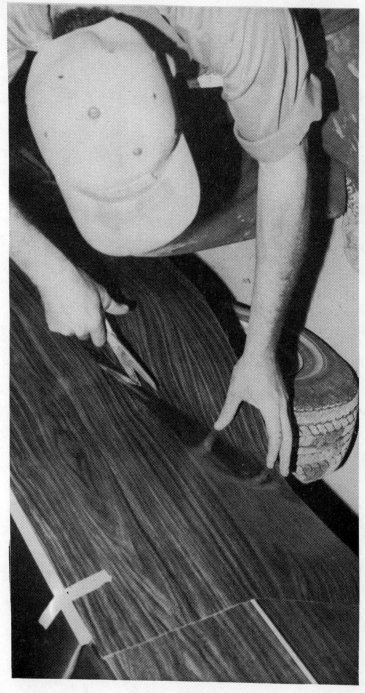

Fig. 15-17. Trim the overlay so that it overlaps the panel edges.

Fig. 15-18. Heat makes the overlay more flexible. (Courtesy Chrysler Corp.)

VINYL ROOF REPAIR

Vinyl roof covers are still popular. With normal care, vinyl will last as long as the paint, but the material is vulnerable to impact damage.

To repair, trim the frayed edges (Figs. 15-21 and 15-22). A gap must be left between edges to be "welded" to allow for expansion and contraction.

Wet a lintless rag with vinyl prep spray (Fig. 15-23) and wipe down the trimmed edges, moving in only one direction (Fig. 15-24).

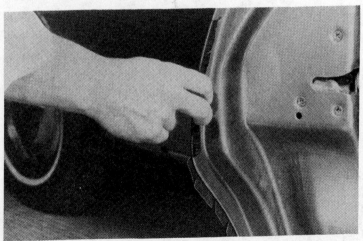

Fig. 15-19. Press the edges down with your fingers, then use a squeegee. (Courtesy Chrysler Corp.)

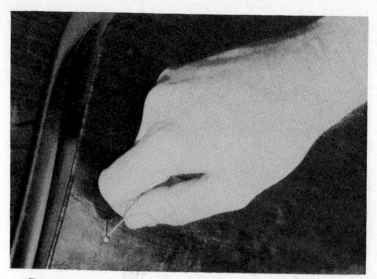

Fig. 15-20. Small bubbles can be punctured. (Courtesy Chrysler Corp.)

Allow the vinyl prep to dry, and, with a small palette, daub vinyl-welding compound on the surface inside the tear. Do not use the compound as a filler—a thin coat is enough. Weld compound is stocked by parts stores and by some car dealers.

Wipe up any compound dribbled on the undamaged vinyl. It will cure and leave a rough finish. Use a heat gun, or, lacking that, a hair

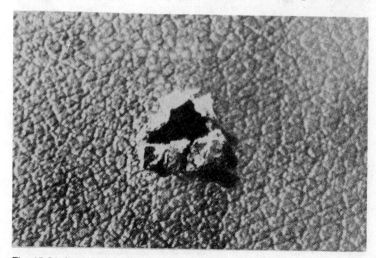

Fig. 15-21. Local damage to vinyl tapes can be repaired. (Courtesy Chrysler Corp.)

Fig. 15-22. The first step is to trim the edges of the tear. (Courtesy Chrysler Corp.)

dryer, and hold it approximately 1 inch from the surface of the compound.

When heated, the edges of the compound tend to rise. Press the compound down with the thumb of your free hand (Fig. 15-25).

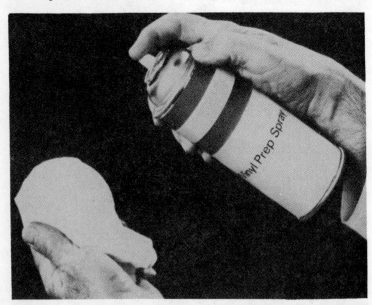

Fig. 15-23. Dampen a clean, lint-free rag with vinyl-prep spray. (Courtesy Chrysler Corp.)

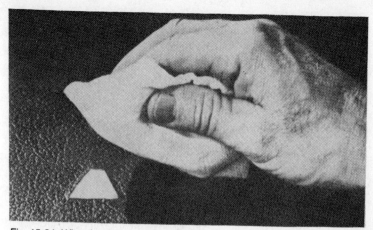

Fig. 15-24. Wipe the damaged area in one direction only. Do not rub back and forth. (Courtesy Chrysler Corp.)

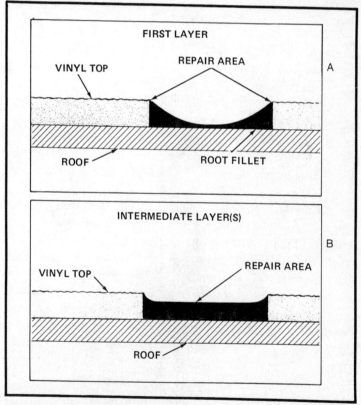

FIRST LAYER

VINYL TOP

REPAIR AREA

A

ROOF

ROOT FILLET

INTERMEDIATE LAYER(S)

B

VINYL TOP

REPAIR AREA

ROOF

Fig. 15-25. As the welding compound is heated, it will buckle in the center (view A); press the edges down with your fingers (view B). (Courtesy Chrysler Corp.)

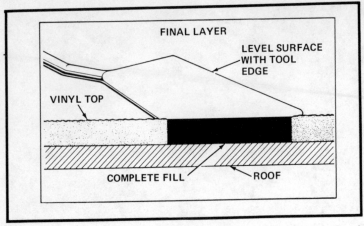

Fig. 15-26. Level the weld with the adjacent vinyl. (Courtesy Chrysler Corp.)

Once pressed down, the compound will remain flat as more heat is applied.

In the initial stages the compound takes on a milky appearance, but it will clear as heat completes the cure. The process should require 10-20 seconds, depending upon the intensity of the heat.

Cool the weld with air from the gun before applying the next coat of compound. If you are in a hurry, you can apply a wet cloth to the weld to speed things up.

Continue to apply and cure successive layers of welding compound. Thin out each layer, or the compound will require excessive heat to cure.

Four welds should bring the repair up to the top of the vinyl, and a palette is used to level the weld flush with the top of the undamaged vinyl (Fig. 15-26). Heat the repair until the adjacent vinyl starts to shine. Remove the heat gun or dryer and implant the crinkle finish with a graining tool. Hold the tool against the weld for at least 5 seconds. Graining tools can be purchased through auto dealers.

Finish the job with liquid vinyl. Spray the first coat on wet, allow 15 minutes to dry, and spray the finish coat. Vinyl will wrinkle as it absorbs the liquid, but will return to normal when the material dries.

Index

staring at Jessie's cap, "is that your good ski cap? What did you do to it?"

"I made a yellow pom-pom," Jessie began. Then she squealed and ran to the window. "Amber's out there! Amber's waiting for me!" She pulled her cap onto her head and ran for the door.

"Hold on a second," laughed Mr. Saunders. "You didn't answer my question. Jessie, do you want to join the den as an honorary member?"

Adam shook his head violently at Jessie.

"No, no, no," he mouthed the words.

Jessie paused, one hand on the doorknob. "No, thank you," she said politely to Mr. Saunders. "Cub Scouts is kind of boring, you know." She tossed her head; her new pom-pom wiggled dangerously. "Well, bye. I've got to go someplace."

Adam let out a huge sigh of relief. He waved cheerfully at Jessie. "Bye! Have a good time!" He started to put back the batteries and the other stuff he'd pulled out of his pocket. His eyes went to the spit wad refrigerator.

"Here," he said in a burst of generosity. "I don't need it anymore. I've got a bubblegum trash can to keep spit wads in." He tossed the little refrigerator toward Jessie.

"Thanks!" Jessie squealed. "Thanks, Adam!" She grabbed the refrigerator and ran out the door, clutching the top of her ski cap to keep the pom-pom in place.

"So long, good-bye, have a good time!" Adam yelled again loudly, happily. He tossed his two batteries high and caught them both.

A wonderful, terrific, free feeling bubbled through him as he watched the door slam and the two yellow pom-pom heads disappear down the sidewalk.

He turned to Mr. Saunders with a grin.

"And what else are we going to do in Cub Scouts this year?"